FOCUS

A 40-DAY DEVOTIONAL

Published by CenterPoint Publishing, publishing.cpchurch.com
98 Jerusalem Ave., Massapequa, NY 11758
www.cpchurch.com

Edited by Nicole Jansezian

Cover and book design by: Kirsten Doukas, pastelblackdesign.com

NAME: _____

START DATE: ___ /___ /___

END DATE: ___ /___ /___

TABLE OF CONTENTS

CALENDAR

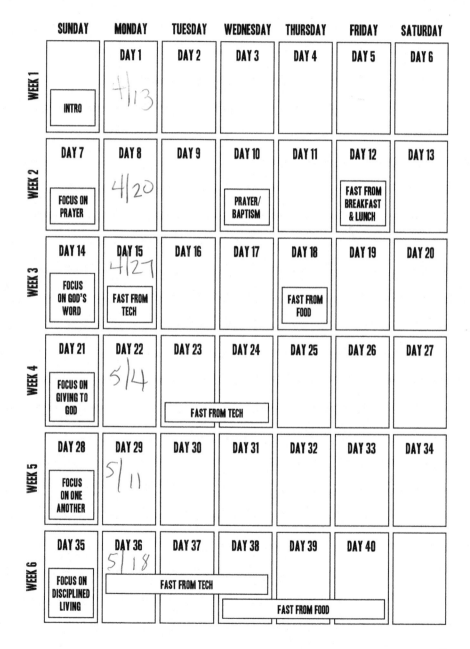

	SUNDAY	MONDAY	TUESDAY	WEDNESDAY	THURSDAY	FRIDAY	SATURDAY
WEEK 1	INTRO	DAY 1 4/13	DAY 2	DAY 3	DAY 4	DAY 5	DAY 6
WEEK 2	DAY 7 FOCUS ON PRAYER	DAY 8 4/20	DAY 9	DAY 10 PRAYER/ BAPTISM	DAY 11	DAY 12 FAST FROM BREAKFAST & LUNCH	DAY 13
WEEK 3	DAY 14 FOCUS ON GOD'S WORD	DAY 15 4/27 FAST FROM TECH	DAY 16	DAY 17	DAY 18 FAST FROM FOOD	DAY 19	DAY 20
WEEK 4	DAY 21 FOCUS ON GIVING TO GOD	DAY 22 5/4	DAY 23 FAST FROM TECH	DAY 24	DAY 25	DAY 26	DAY 27
WEEK 5	DAY 28 FOCUS ON ONE ANOTHER	DAY 29 5/11	DAY 30	DAY 31	DAY 32	DAY 33	DAY 34
WEEK 6	DAY 35 FOCUS ON DISCIPLINED LIVING	DAY 36 5/18 FAST FROM TECH	DAY 37	DAY 38 FAST FROM FOOD	DAY 39	DAY 40	

FORWARD

by Brian McMillan

I am so excited that you have decided to join us on this 40-day journey as we focus on getting to know God better.

As Richard Foster writes in Celebration of Discipline, "Superficiality is the curse of the age. The doctrine of instant satisfaction is a primary spiritual problem. The desperate need today is not for a greater number of intelligent people, or gifted people, but for deep people. The classic disciplines of the spiritual life calls us to move beyond the surface living into the depths. They invite us to explore the inner caverns of the spiritual realm."

This is the third time in 13 years that we have taken on writing a devotional for our church on spiritual development. And every time our church has deliberately engaged with God on a deeper level, we have been transformed. That's what happens when you spend time with Jesus. You change.

This time I asked members of our staff to write the different days of this devotional. I am so proud of them! I am touched by how they poured themselves into their individual pieces and shared their hearts and experiences. Their distinct personalities have come through in each of their writings. That being said, none of us are professional writers. I am sure you can find better devotionals out there! But these 40 devotionals deal with topics God has challenged us with as a church for a season such as this. They are personal.

So please take the time to participate.

And for those who got this book from a friend or took a chance and bought it at a garage sale, I hope it blesses you and helps bring you to a better knowledge of God.

Enjoy getting your spiritual life into focus!

WEEK 1

INTRODUCTION

DAY 1

GET FOCUSED

by Brian McMillan, Lead Pastor

SCRIPTURE VERSE

"And let us run with perseverance the race marked out for us, fixing our eyes on Jesus, the pioneer and perfecter of faith." Hebrews 12:1-2

DEVOTIONAL

We have all taken blurry pictures at one time or another. Usually, in our rush to capture the moment we don't give enough time for our camera (or phone) to bring the scene into focus. We are left with an ambiguous blur, with colors and indistinct shapes hinting at what the picture was supposed to look like. In all likelihood, without the distinct lines and details of the photo we wanted, we will delete it. Why? Because no one can appreciate a picture that you can't see.

Focus is important. Details are important.

Sometimes we move too much and too fast that we can't really get a sharp picture of God in our lives. For many of us, he is simply a blur. We think we can see him in the picture of our existence, but then again, we really aren't sure.

Friends, this doesn't have to be!

God has created us in such a way that we should be able to really know him. To hear his voice. To feel his touch. To see his leading. To see him clearly.

Yet, for many of us, the picture of God in our lives is out of focus and we are unsure how to resolve this. The cares and busyness of life distract us from taking the time to focus in on God.

This is why we are going on this journey over the next 40 days. Let this devotional be either a beginner's guide, or an intentional reminder of how to focus in on Jesus so that we see him clearly. Over these next 40 days we are going to look at different practices, often called spiritual disciplines or spiritual formation, that God has given us.

Each day will include a Bible verse that we encourage you to contemplate and memorize, a devotional, a short Bible study, life application questions and a guided prayer.

Our hope is that after 40 days of intentionally focusing on God through this devotional, our Sunday messages, small group discussions and practicing certain spiritual disciplines, that the picture of God will become abundantly clear in all of our lives!

BIBLE STUDY

Read Psalm 63. (If you don't own a Bible go to www.biblegateway.com)

1. What are the words that David uses to describe seeking after God?

_____

_____

_____

2. What have been the biggest hindrances for you spending time with God?

_____

_____

_____

_____

DAY 1

PERSONAL APPLICATION

1. When are you going to spend time doing this devotional? Be specific!

_____

_____

2. What are you hoping to get out of these 40 days?

_____

_____

_____

CLOSING PRAYER

At the end of each devotional we have added a guided prayer. These prayers give you a starting place to come before God. Then try to continue to pray for 5 or more minutes.

God, help me to focus on you over these nexct 40 days. Open my eyes. Help me to see you.

DAY 2

WHY WE WERE CREATED

by Brian McMillan, Lead Pastor

SCRIPTURE VERSE

"Everyone who is called by my name, whom I created for my glory, whom I formed and made." Isaiah 43:7

DEVOTIONAL

Everything created throughout history has been invented with a specific purpose in mind. For example, if you try to drive a guitar to work you won't get far. A guitar is clearly designed to make music. If you try to cook a steak on your television set, you can expect a raw, cold meal. If you attempt to call someone with your lamp…Yep, you get the point. Anything anyone has created has an intended purpose. And it's only when it's being used for that purpose that it makes sense and actually works.

We are no different! God created us with a specific purpose in mind, mainly to know and worship him.

"But you are a chosen people, a royal priesthood, a holy nation, *God's special possession, that you may declare the praises of him who called* you out of darkness into his wonderful light." 1 Peter 1:9

"For in him all things were created: things in heaven and on earth, visible and invisible, whether thrones or powers or rulers or authorities; *all things have been created through him and for him.*" Colossians 1:16

These are just two of many Bible verses that tell us that we are God's special possession and that we were created for him. Don't miss this: The God of

DAY 2

the universe cares about you! He made you. He knows you. He loves you. And here is the greatest part—he wants you to know him.

It stands to reason that unless we are functioning within our intended, created purpose, something in our lives would be amiss. Sort of like trying to take a bath in the dishwasher. That's simply not the purpose of a dishwasher.

Until our relationship with Jesus becomes a real part of our daily lives, we will miss out on what it means to really live. God has created us with the ability to think, reason and be relational. He designed us so that we could love him, talk to him and worship him. Our relationship with him is the greatest we can and will ever have. And through that relationship we fulfill the greatest purpose of our lives.

Live the life that you were designed to live!

BIBLE STUDY

We can have a relationship with God because Jesus made the way through his atoning sacrifice on the cross. To explain this process, many Christians share what is often referred to as the "Romans Road." Take some time to walk through the five steps that the Apostle Paul outlines in the Book of Romans and write down what each verse means to you.

1. Romans 3:10-12, 23

_____

_____

_____

2. Romans 6:23

_____

_____

_____

3. Romans 5:8

_____

_____

_____

4. Romans 10:9-10, 13

_____

_____

_____

5. Romans 5:1, 8:1, 8:38-39

_____

_____

_____

PERSONAL APPLICATION

If you don't think you have ever asked Jesus to forgive you of your sins, why wait another minute? If this applies to you, pray the following prayer.

CLOSING PRAYER

Dear Lord Jesus, I know that I am a sinner, and I ask for your forgiveness. I believe you died for my sins and rose from the dead. I turn from my sins and invite you to come into my heart and life. I want to trust and follow you as my Lord and Savior. In your name, Amen.

Now email me so I can pray for you and celebrate with you!
brian@cpchurch.com

DAY 3

PRONE TO DRIFT AWAY

by Henry Fuhrman, Executive Pastor of Ministries

SILENCE

Begin your time with two minutes of silence and stillness before God. This will help you clear your head of all the distractions of your day and center your thoughts on the Lord.

SCRIPTURE VERSE

"We must pay the most careful attention to what we have heard, so that we do not drift away." Hebrews 2:1

DEVOTIONAL

The writer of Hebrews tells us something very significant about what it means to follow Jesus. According to this passage, being a Christian means being watchful and attentive to the truth of God. If we fail to be mindful of what we have heard, we will inevitably "drift away."

This phrase "drift away" literally means to be "carried past a thing" and to "miss it completely." Picture yourself in a raft headed downstream in a river, but without paddles. Without paddles, it's impossible to guide the raft. Without paddles, it's impossible to avoid rocks, trees or other dangerous objects. Without paddles you cannot stop, slow down or change direction. Without paddles, I am not getting into this raft (I'm just saying!). Being on a raft without paddles means I have absolutely no control, but will end up wherever the current takes me.

Creating spiritual discipline in our walk with God is like using paddles while on a raft. Our lives are being pulled by currents that move, both within us and around us. Our hearts are, by nature, prone to drift away from the Lord (Jeremiah 17:9) and the things of the world often pull us away from doing the will of God in our lives (1 John 2:15-17). Unless we are awake, alert and mindful of what God has told us, it will be impossible to follow Jesus. Without a thoughtful, intentional and vigilant plan for following Jesus, the currents that surround us will inevitably "carry us past" the life that God has for us, we will "miss it completely."

Consider the following words from Eugene Peterson in *The Pastor*:

> *"I love being an American. I love this place in which I have been placed—its language, its history its energy. But I don't love 'the American way,' its culture and values. I don't love the rampant consumerism that treats God as a product to be marketed. I don't love the dehumanizing ways that turn men, women and children into impersonal roles and causes and statistics. I don't love the competitive spirit that treats others as rivals and even as enemies. The cultural conditions in which I am immersed require, at least for me, a kind of fierce vigilance to guard my vocation from those cultural pollutants so dangerously toxic to persons who want to follow Jesus in the way that he is Jesus. I wanted my life, both my personal and working life, to be shaped by God and the scriptures and prayer."*

BIBLE STUDY

1. Read Jeremiah 17 and Psalm 51. Reflect on the nature of the human heart. What do the writers teach about the natural condition and inclination of our hearts?

_____

_____

2. Read 1 John 2:15-17. How do the "things of the world" pull you away from following God?

_____

_____

DAY 3

PERSONAL APPLICATION

1. How has your own heart pulled you away from God?

_____

_____

2. Describe how external factors in your work/culture/environment have tugged you away from God?

_____

_____

3. What are some ways you can be "fiercely vigilant" in steering your own heart toward God?

_____

_____

4. What are some ways you can be "fiercely vigilant" in following God in your work/culture/environment?

_____

_____

CLOSING PRAYER

Father God, it is my desire that you be the primary force of my life. Direct me, lead me, pull me closer to you. And as the Psalmist prays, so do I: *"Guide me in your truth* and teach me, for you are God my Savior, and my hope is in you all day long." (Psalm 25:5)

DAY 4

CONNECTING TO THE HOLY SPIRIT

by Brian McMillan, Lead Pastor

SCRIPTURE VERSE

"All this I have spoken while still with you. But the Advocate, the Holy Spirit, whom the Father will send in my name, will *teach* you all things and will *remind* you of everything I have said to you." John 14:25-26

DEVOTIONAL

As Jesus spoke these words he knew his time on earth was coming to an end and that the cross was drawing near. He also knew that his disciples would soon be confused and scared. And rightfully so! They would wonder how they would continue without their leader, what would become of them or whether one of them would be next to die on a cross.

So Jesus promised his disciples that they would not be alone and that another would come in his place.

I wonder if the disciples were disappointed with this news. I mean, they were with *Jesus!* What could be better than that? Who could take his place in their lives? They couldn't understand what Jesus meant until they met the person of whom he was speaking. In Acts 2, we read about the day of Pentecost. On this day, the disciples met the Holy Spirit. The Holy Spirit, the third person of the trinity, filled them. The disciples, in that moment, knew that God was now living in them and their spirits came alive. From that moment, a new power was birthed in the church—that of God dwelling *in* his people.

In 1 Corinthians 6:19, Paul writes, "Do you not know that your bodies are

DAY 4

temples of the Holy Spirit, who is in you, whom you have received from God?" Every Christian has access to God through the Holy Spirit—he lives in us. He becomes part of us. And as Jesus said in John 14, the Holy Spirit now teaches us and reminds us of the truth of Christ.

But often we don't know he dwells in us because we don't hear him. We don't feel him. We don't sense him. That is not how the Christian life should be! We should live in such a way that the Holy Spirit noticeably influences us and guides our faith. Through the Holy Spirit we grow in the likeness of God. God wants to be active in our lives!

Doesn't that sound awesome?

For this to happen, we need to proactively seek him. We must desire to hear from God and be willing to pick up the phone and dial his number. This is what we pray will happen for you over the next 37 days. As you use this devotional, open your Bible and spend time in prayer, we hope you make space in your life to connect with God. The more time you spend in the presence of God, the more you will create the space you need to hear the Holy Spirit.

BIBLE STUDY

Read Romans 8:1-17.

1.   When you feel the struggle within you between the flesh and the spirit, do you consider the spiritual significance of it?

_____

2.   How can you be more intentional in trying to hear God within that struggle?

_____

_____

_____

_____

3. List a few things that the apostle Paul explains to us about what the Holy Spirit means for our lives.

_____

_____

_____

PERSONAL APPLICATION

Take a few moments and write down the thoughts and ideas that you think God is impressing to you through the Holy Spirit.

_____

_____

_____

_____

_____

CLOSING PRAYER

God, I recognize that I need to hear your voice. Help me to discern how you are challenging me. Help me to be open to your working in my life. Holy Spirit, I need more. Amen

DAY 5

WHAT IS PRAYER?

by John Ulin, Pastor of Discipleship and Spiritual Formation

SCRIPTURE VERSE

"May my prayer be set before you like incense; may the lifting up of my hands be like the evening sacrifice." Psalm 141:2

SILENCE

Take two minutes to quietly reflect on this verse.

DEVOTIONAL

During my time in sales I made thousands of phone calls. This had to be one of the most difficult jobs: I had about three seconds to get a person interested in what I was selling. Most people hung up on me. Occasionally someone cursed at me, and then hung up. So when I finally did get someone who would give me a moment of their time it was such a relief. I was grateful that someone, who presumably had lots to do, could find some time to speak with me.

Prayer, if I may define it simply, is conversation with God. Read that sentence again. Prayer is a conversation with the maker of heaven and earth. The King of Kings. The Lord of Lords. And we get to have a conversation with him! How incredible is that? One of Jesus' preeminent teachings on prayer comes in Matthew 6:9-13:

> "Pray, then, in this way:
> 'Our Father who is in heaven,
> Hallowed be Your name.

Your kingdom come.
Your will be done,
On earth as it is in heaven.
Give us this day our daily bread.
And forgive us our debts, as we also have forgiven our debtors.
And do not lead us into temptation, but deliver us from evil. For
Yours is the kingdom and the power and the glory forever. Amen.'"

The Lord's Prayer, as it is commonly known, covers three of the five main activities within prayer: praise ("hallowed be your name"), confession ("forgive us") and supplication, or asking for provision ("daily bread," "deliver us"). This prayer was not meant to be the only one we pray, but rather a template to keep our dialogue with God balanced.

The fourth activity in prayer is thanksgiving. This aspect is prevalent throughout the Bible, especially in the Psalms (106:1; 107:1; 136:1; etc.) and prayers of Paul (Philippians 1:3; Colossians 1:3; etc.).

The final aspect of prayer is listening. A friendship would not last long if only one party spoke. In Psalm 62:5 the writer declares, "My soul waits in silence for God alone; for my hope is in Him." God may want to speak to us through his Spirit during prayer, but it can be difficult to hear him if we keep talking.

Maybe you've never prayed before. If so, here's what I recommend: Say the Lord's Prayer every day. After you become familiar with it, you can add your own need in place of "daily bread" and you can tell him that you're thankful for something specific he's done for you.

Lastly, surround yourself with people who pray. Listen to them. Don't copy them, but take note of how they address God and express their praise. In doing so, your own prayers will evolve naturally into something unique between you and God.

It is easy to take for granted the invitation to "boldly approach" his throne. These days, it is so hard to get a few moments of someone's time and, yet God has made a way, through Christ, for us to speak with him. What an incredible gift!

DAY 5

Prayer is far more than just asking God for stuff (supplication). It is a discipline wherein we listen for his voice, ask for his forgiveness and give him thanksgiving and praise because his love endures forever.

BIBLE STUDY

1. Read Matthew 6:9-15. Do you usually begin your prayers with giving glory to God?

_____

2. Is confessing your sin to God a regular part of your prayers?

_____

3. Explain the role of forgiveness in this prayer, specifically considering verses 14 and 15.

_____

_____

_____

PERSONAL APPLICATION

1. Before you pray, reflect on whether you need to ask anyone for forgiveness.

2. In your prayer, ask God to help you forgive someone who hurt you.

CLOSING PRAYER

Heavenly Father, I praise you for your goodness to me. Thank you for sending your Son to take away my sin, so that I could come before you in prayer. Help me to see prayer as communion with you, the creator of heaven and earth, and not just an exercise in rattling off of my needs. Lord, let me desire to pray regularly and to pray for the things that honor you. I worship you. Amen.

DAY 6

DEVOTED TO PRAYER

by Brian McMillan, Lead Pastor

SCRIPTURE VERSE

"Devote yourselves to *prayer,* being watchful and thankful." Colossians 4:2

DEVOTIONAL

Pastor Bill Hybels has a book whose title always grabs me. It's called *Too Busy NOT to Pray.* It is a reminder that in our busy lives we need to be intentional to carve out time that we spend with God in prayer.

If prayer is communicating with God, then we should want to do our part in reaching out to him everyday. Philippians 4:6 says, "Do not be anxious about anything, *but in every situation, by prayer and petition,* with thanksgiving, present your requests to God." We are challenged to maintain a posture of prayer in every situation. Clearly, prayer is meant to be a priority in our lives.

Oswald Chambers wrote, "Prayer does not fit us for the greater work; prayer is the greater work." Prayer isn't simply something we do, it's what we are. As Christians we should be a people *of* prayer.

Yet the intentional posture of prayer often escapes us. In the midst of our hectic day, many of us throw out a quick "Hail Mary" prayer: *"God, get me through this day!"* And then we move on. But our prayer lives must be so much more if we are to know God!

Many would believe that pastors spend much of their time reading the Bible and praying. I wish that were true. If I may share with you a confession, this often is not the case with me. Between counseling, overseeing staff, ADD, message preparation, emails, phone calls, ADD, building repair, ADD, church finances, board meetings and all of the other thousands of tasks that pop up, I struggle to find the time to pray.

With busyness comes anxiety. With anxiety comes a lack of productivity. A lack of productivity creates more anxiety, which further hinders my productivity...which causes more anxiety. Can you relate to this? Yet Paul exhorts, "Do not be anxious about anything!"

Our fast paced lives and subsequent anxiety become an excuse for not praying. Yet it is in these busy, anxious, stressed moments of life that we need God the most! We need God's peace. We need his wisdom (James 1:5). We need his power. And we gain these through prayer.

Friends, we can't allow busyness to be the reason that we don't pray or practice any of the spiritual disciplines. The more responsibilities we have, the more we need God. As life becomes more hectic, we should become more persistent in finding time to pray.

You wouldn't unplug your computer when the battery is low. And so we must not unplug from God when life gets busy. It is only through prayer that we will be able to make it!

BIBLE STUDY 4:2-6

Read Colossians 4:2-6.

1. What would a life devoted to prayer look like to you?

_____

_____

2. What does Paul say that prayer can accomplish?

_____

_____

PERSONAL APPLICATION

I have often found it very helpful to write down the things I pray for so that I can see God's faithfulness through the years. Find a place, maybe in the back of your Bible or in a separate notebook to write the things for which you are praying. Make sure you date them. Then keep returning to these to see how God has answered your prayers.

CLOSING PRAYER

God help me to be a person of prayer. Help me to not let my busyness become an excuse, but rather, when I get busy, compel me to seek you even more. Help me to overcome anxiety as I trust in you and bring my petitions before you. Amen.

WEEK 2

FOCUS ON PRAYER

DAY 7

POWER OF PRAYER

by Brian McMillan, Lead Pastor

SCRIPTURE VERSE

"This is the confidence we have in approaching God: that if we ask anything according to his will, he hears us. And if we know that he hears us—whatever we ask—we know that we have what we asked of him." 1 John 5:14-15

DEVOTIONAL

What an exciting verse! If we ask according to God's will, he will deliver! Of course the stipulation here is "according to God's will." Just because you want something doesn't mean it's good for you or that God wants you to have it. But John is letting the church know that we need to ask and then God hears us and moves on our behalf. Jesus says a similar thing in Matthew 7:8: "For everyone who asks receives." Note that both verses stress one key word:

Ask.

How do we ask? Through prayer.

It's through prayer that a Christian experiences the hand of God in his or her life. When I pray, God moves powerfully on my behalf. When I don't pray or ask, I don't receive. I often wonder how our lives would be different if we were to cry out to God more often. Imagine if we, corporately or individually, really acted as if we had a direct line to an omnipotent God who is able to do immeasurably more than all we ask or imagine, according to his power (Ephesians 3:20). Life would look a lot different.

Even as I was writing this, I paused to ask God for his power in my life. I repented for trying to live through my own strength and for my pride in not wanting anyone's help, including God's. When I think of the work that God wants to do through us, and yet I see how little he seems to move in our lives, I'm convinced it's because he is simply waiting for us to ask, to be persistent (Luke 18:1-8), to be bold.

If we are not in prayer, then we are spiritually powerless.

So may we increase our faith. May we see our prayers as petitions before the king of the universe!

BIBLE STUDY

Read James 5:13-18.

1. What are some of the things that James is challenging the church to do in prayer?

_____

_____

_____

_____

2. Sometimes when we pray we don't get the answers we hoped to receive. How do the verses in this devotional challenge our understanding of God's response to us?

_____

_____

_____

_____

DAY 7

PERSONAL APPLICATION

1. What bold prayers have you recently prayed and how has God responded?

_____

_____

_____

_____

_____

2. What bold prayer requests can you bring before God today?

_____

_____

_____

_____

_____

_____

CLOSING PRAYER

Heavenly father, thank you for the gift of prayer. Thank you for hearing every word and every thought that I pray to you. God, show me your will. Teach me your ways so that my prayers will be aligned with your heart. Amen.

DAY 8

CORPORATE PRAYER

by Anthony Bonura, Pastor of Congregational Care

SCRIPTURE VERSE

"After they prayed, the place where they were meeting was shaken and they were all filled with the Holy Spirit and spoke the Word of God boldly." Acts 4:31

DEVOTIONAL

Have you ever been to an event, whether a game or a concert, that drew a large crowd of people? The massive amount of people generates high noise levels at these events. I remember being at a playoff game for the Mets and the stadium was filled to capacity. When the fans cheered I actually felt the stadium rocking! The power of this many people joining together can impact the players and even the outcome of the game. So it is with corporate prayer.

The Apostle Paul knew the power of corporate prayer and he often depended upon the prayers of the church for his ministry. In Ephesians 6:19, Paul asks the church for prayer that he may fearlessly preach the gospel. Paul once again asks for prayer that he will be able to proclaim the gospel clearly (Colossians 4:2-4). Paul also asks the church to pray that he would be delivered from evil and wicked men who do not share the faith (2 Thessalonians 3:2).

Peter and John also depended upon corporate prayer. In Acts 4, Peter and John joined in with the church to pray for greater power and ability to share the gospel. In Acts 12:1-11, when Peter was arrested by King Herod, the church earnestly prayed to God for his release. In response to these cor-

DAY 8

porate prayers, God released Peter from that prison cell. This is the power of corporate prayer.

What does all this mean for us? We should pray corporately. We should pray that our leaders would have the ability to share the Word of God fearlessly and with clarity. We should pray for one another that we would be delivered from evil. Pray always and without ceasing with one mind and one purpose that we would see the gospel advance in our time.

BIBLE STUDY

In Acts 12 we see the powerful effect of corporate prayer. King Herod arrested some who belonged to the church in order to persecute them. He had James the brother of John put to death and when he saw this pleased the Jews he had Peter seized and thrown into prison. This was a time where corporate prayer was needed.

Read the account in Acts 12.

1. Write down or highlight the chain of events that occurred in direct response to the church's prayers for Peter in Acts 12:5.

_____

_____

_____

_____

2. What was their reaction when they saw Peter?

_____

_____

_____

PERSONAL APPLICATION

This Wednesday is our monthly Night of Prayer and Worship. Put the date in your calendar now and do your best to attend.

CLOSING PRAYER

Lord, I thank you for the power of corporate prayer. I see now that it has the power to strengthen each of us in the sharing of our faith. Going forward, may I join with others in prayer.

DAY 9

PRAYER WITHOUT CEASING

by Nachbi Lacossiere, Director of College and Career Ministries

REFLECTION

Jesus, free me of any distractions that may be pulling me from you in this time. May your word resonate deep within me for my own sake and for the world around me.

SCRIPTURE VERSE

"Pray continually, give thanks in all circumstances; for this is the will of God in Christ Jesus for you." 1 Thessalonians 5:17-18

DEVOTIONAL

I loved to play basketball when I was growing up. But after a terrible play on my part, my coach would warn me, "Nachbi, you better make sure you practice and work on your game every day. Don't play video games all day." It was clear to both of us that I wasn't practicing the way that I should have been. I noticed a huge difference in my game when I devoted myself to practice and when I did not. When I practiced daily, I was confident and prepared at game time. As a competitor I didn't like to lose, but at least I could be satisfied with my effort and preparation.

Just as I felt confident when I practiced daily, I get that same assurance from God when I pray continually. Prayer gives us the confidence to come before the Father. It involves giving thanks in all circumstances. Praying enables us to maintain communion with Jesus and deepen our love for him. To love Jesus is to love prayer because prayer keeps us close to him. It sustains us. It keeps us in the will of God. It keeps us in the game, so to speak.

Ceasing to pray means ceasing all of the above. We don't give thanks or maintain our fellowship with God. Without thanksgiving, we become entitled and where there is entitlement, there is no room for prayer. Where there is pride, there is no room for prayer. And where there is no room for prayer there is no room for God.

When we reach a point where aren't in our game in our prayer lives, we may feel like we have failed or we can't be forgiven. But God doesn't condemn us. Even when we turn from him, he stands patiently with his arms wide open saying, "Come to me, you who are weary and burdened, and I will give you rest."

There is power in your prayers. Even if you feel God hasn't heard you, he has and he will respond. Continue to pray and you will experience God in a deeper and more profound way.

BIBLE STUDY

1. Psalm 145:18 says, "The Lord is near to all who call on him, to all who call on him in truth." Do you call (or pray) to the Lord enough to where he feels close to you? When you pray to the Lord, are you saying what you think he wants to hear or you speaking the truth in your heart?

_____

_____

_____

_____

PERSONAL APPLICATION

1. In what areas of my life can I pray more?

_____

_____

_____

DAY 9

2. What drives my prayers—getting something from God or getting in touch with him?

_____

_____

_____

3. What in my day-to-day routine keeps me from praying?

_____

_____

_____

CLOSING PRAYER

Jesus, help me to have the desire and discipline to pray continually. Draw me close to your heart and keep me humble to seek you all of my days. Amen!

DAY 10

THE PSALMS: OUR SCHOOL OF PRAYER

by Henry Fuhrman, Executive Pastor of Ministries

SILENCE

Begin your time with two minutes of silence and stillness before God. This will help clear your head of all the distractions of your day and center your thoughts on the Lord.

SCRIPTURE VERSE

"Lord, teach us to pray." Luke 11:1

DEVOTIONAL

God invites us to spend time with him in communion and conversation and to make our requests known to Him (Philippians 4:6). Although this is a key component of prayer, communion with God entails so much more than simply offering our personal requests to Him. God is not to be treated like a genie in a bottle or like Santa Claus who receives our wish lists and responds with gifts.

In prayer, we are invited to lay our entire lives before God, not just our needs. In prayer, we come before God in adoration, worship and praise. We confess our sins and ask for forgiveness. We thank God for who He is and for how He loves and provides for us. We intercede on behalf of others, asking God to intervene for those in need and to implore Him to execute justice in the world. While we certainly can submit individual requests, we should take the opportunity to truly commune with God, to share all that is on our hearts and to know all that is on His.

DAY 10

Perhaps the best way to learn to pray is to attend the "School of Prayer" located in the Bible. The book of Psalms is really a compilation of prayers. Praying the Psalms is one of the best ways to learn to pray. The Psalms have served as a hymnal in synagogues for centuries and were almost certainly prayed by Jesus and the early Christians. For many people, the Psalms have provided language for some of our deepest emotions and have demonstrated how to bare our souls before God. Indeed, the Psalms "become like a mirror to the person singing them" (St. Athanasius) and provide a model for how to approach God even through life's most difficult moments.

Consider the following words from Dietrich Bonhoeffer:

> *"If we wish to pray with confidence and gladness, then the words of the Holy Scripture will have to be the solid basis of our prayer. For here we know that Jesus Christ, the Word of God, teaches us to pray. The words which come from God become, then, the steps on which we find our way to God."*

BIBLE STUDY

Read the Psalms listed below and offer them up as a personal prayer to God:

Psalms of Adoration: Psalm 150
Key verse: "Let everything that has breath praise the LORD."

Psalms of Confession: Psalm 32
Key verse: "I will confess my transgressions…and you forgave the guilt of my sin."

Psalms of Thanksgiving: Psalm 146
Key verse: "Enter his gates with thanksgiving and his courts with praise."

Psalms of Intercession: Psalm 85
Key verse: "Restore us again, God our Savior."

Psalms of Supplication: Psalm 86
Key verse: "Teach me your way, LORD, that I may rely on your faithfulness."

PERSONAL APPLICATION

1. Many have noticed that the Psalms might be categorized as different types of prayers to God. There are Psalms of Adoration, Confession, Thanksgiving, Intercession and Supplication. Which of the following "categories of prayer" appears most in your prayer life?

_____

_____

2. How might God be calling you to expand your prayers to Him?

_____

_____

_____

_____

CLOSING PRAYER

Heavenly Father, my prayer to you today is the same as the Psalmist from years ago: "May the words of my mouth and the meditations of my heart be pleasing in your sight, Lord, my Rock and my Redeemer." (Psalm 19:14)

DAY 11

FASTING WITH A PURPOSE

by Brian McMillan, Lead Pastor

SCRIPTURE VERSE

"Man shall not live on bread alone, but on every word that comes from the mouth of God." Matthew 4:4

DEVOTIONAL

This is not a devotional on weight loss! I'm sure some of you are thinking that if you could lose a few pounds while incorporating something spiritual, great! But this mindset could actually detract from spiritual reasons for fasting.

The purpose of fasting is to abstain from something physical, usually food, in order to focus more intentionally on God.

Even though the Bible doesn't command us to fast, we see it being practiced often. In Matthew 6:16, Jesus talks about fasting for God and not for the praise of people. He starts off by saying, "*When* you fast…" not *if* or *maybe*. Fasting was a common practice in spiritual development. It was assumed in Jesus' day that anyone seeking God would practice fasting. Further we see the church fasting corporately in Acts 13:2 as they are seek God in making some important decisions. Fasting and prayer often are associated with each other.

Many times in my life when I felt I needed real clarity from God, I fasted and prayed. Before I started the church, I sought God's wisdom through fasting in order to make sure I was supposed to take this step. Before I proposed to Sarah, I fasted. During periods of spiritual oppression in the church, I fasted and prayed for God's protection and victory. Each of these fasts looked different. Sometimes I abstained from breakfast, others time from certain foods and yet others were from all food altogether. The length of time also varied from one day to several weeks.

The first few times I fasted, the only thing I noticed was that I was hungry! But with time and practice, fasting has become a real way for me to seek God and focus on things of the Spirit. It helps me to hear the voice of God more clearly.

But like all spiritual formation practices, we need to make sure we are doing them for the right reasons. John Calvin said that, "God does not greatly esteem fasting of itself, unless an inner emotion of the heart is present and true displeasure at one's sin, true humility, and true sorrowing arising from the fear of God. Indeed, fasting is not otherwise useful then when it is joined as a lesser help to these."

Part of this devotional experience includes fasting. Our first fast is tomorrow and we will forgo breakfast. Use the time you would normally eat to spend some more time in prayer and contemplation. When you hear your stomach grumble, take that moment to praise God for all that he has given you.

When you fast, you narrow the focus of your life to the frequency of God. So stay tuned, and listen in.

BIBLE STUDY

1. Read Isaiah 58. Why was God dissatisfied with the fasting practiced by his people?

_____

_____

_____

_____

DAY 11

2. What must we do to bring about God's blessing?

_____

_____

_____

PERSONAL APPLICATION

1. What makes you most nervous about fasting?

_____

_____

_____

2. How would you describe a proper attitude to be kept throughout a fast?

_____

_____

_____

CLOSING PRAYER

God, as I fast help me to hear your voice. Give me strength when I am hungry or weak. God, as I abstain from physical sustenance, will you build me up spiritually so that I can tune in to your voice? Amen.

DAY 12

THE DOS AND DON'TS OF FASTING

by Brian McMillan, Lead Pastor

SCRIPTURE VERSE

"How much better to get wisdom than gold, to get insight rather than silver!" Proverbs 16:16

DEVOTIONAL

From my experience with and study of fasting, I have come up with some guidelines that have shaped how I challenge people to fast. These concepts help us get the most out of fasting while keeping us safe. We must understand the potential physical, emotional and spiritual consequences of fasting without wisdom. And before we go into our first food fast, we must take the time to process these six suggestions:

1. MAKE SURE THAT YOU ARE PHYSICALLY AND MENTALLY AT A POINT THAT YOU CAN FAST.

Physically: I appreciate people's desire to live for the fullness of God. But sometimes our bodies can work against us. If you have any physical condition that might prevent you from fasting, for example if you are sick, taking medication that must be taken with food, are pregnant or breast feeding, please do not attempt a food fast until you have first spoken with your doctor. You're not being "spiritual" when you don't use the wisdom God has given you. If you are unable to participate in a full abstaining from food during a fast, you can be creative to achieve the same goal. For example, you can limit what you eat or maintain a bland diet that will allow for your mind and heart to focus on God during the fast.

Mentally: We must address a realistic concern affecting both men and

DAY 12

women. Billboards, commercials and magazines dictate to the American public what everyone should look like. Because of that, many people have skewed, unrealistic self-images and have become obsessed with their bodies. People feel compelled to unrealistically look like airbrushed, Photoshop-enhanced models and actors. This leaves people feeling discouraged, unattractive and depressed. As a result, millions of Americans struggle with eating disorders such as bulimia and anorexia.

These illnesses are just as prevalent in the church. That's why whenever we talk about fasting we must add a very important warning with the teaching: *If you have struggled with an eating disorder, do not fast from food!* This does not reflect a lack of spirituality or a poor walk with God. Rather this is an opportunity to implement wisdom in dealing with an illness with which you struggle.

2. IF YOU HAVE NEVER FASTED BEFORE, TAKE YOUR TIME!

Don't jump into a week-long fast the first time you plan to abstain from food. We are beginning with a one-day fast and slowly working our way to a three-day fast. This will give you a chance to know how your body will react so that you can stay focused on the spiritual matters at hand.

3. MAKE SURE YOU DRINK A LOT OF WATER WHEN YOU FAST.

Staying hydrated is crucial. Fasting from food doesn't mean fasting from water. And while you're at it, try to refrain from beverages that are high in sugar or caffeine, which are dehydrating. Keep it simple.

4. KEEP THE FOCUS ON GOD.

One time when I was fasting, I lost focus. It stopped being about God and ended up being a competition with myself to see how long I could go without eating. I lost the whole purpose of fasting in the first place! As soon as I realized that, I ended the fast. If the fast isn't about God, stop.

5. STICK IT OUT.

For healthy people, the human body can easily go several days without food. You might feel strange because you have never done it before, but you'll be fine. Don't let hunger overpower you. I have found that the first day or two is always the most difficult. I'm sure that by dinner you'll be ready to eat anything. But all of our fasts in this devotional are relatively short, so stick with it; you'll be glad you did.

6. COME BACK EASY.

My first reaction when I come off a fast is to have the equivalent of Thanksgiving dinner and stuff as much food in my mouth as possible. But I haven't fasted to draw close to God just so that I can rationalize gluttony. It's actually very unhealthy to gorge oneself right after a fast. So when you do come off a fast, start with small, simple meals. Let your body adjust to food before you fill it back up.

I hope and pray that fasting gives you another tool you can use to connect with God.

BIBLE STUDY

1. Read over these passages on fasting and list the purpose of each fast.

•   Acts 13:1-3

_____

_____

_____

•   Acts 14:21-23

_____

_____

_____

•   Judges 20:26-28

_____

_____

_____

DAY 12

- 1 Samuel 7:1-6

_____

_____

_____

PERSONAL APPLICATION

1. What are you hoping to get out of fasting?

_____

_____

_____

2. List three things you are going to be praying about while you fast.

_____

_____

_____

CLOSING PRAYER

God I seek your wisdom with fasting. If I shouldn't fast from food, may I have the courage to admit it. May this time of fasting draw me to you. Amen.

DAY 13

FASTING BEYOND FOOD

by Brian McMillan, Lead Pastor

SCRIPTURE VERSE

"For it is God who works in you to will and to act in order to fulfill his good purpose." Philippians 2:13

DEVOTIONAL

As I shared on Day 12, the purpose of fasting is to deny oneself something physical in order to focus on the spiritual. We can fast from a variety of things beyond food for a variety of reasons. Take for example 1 Corinthians 7:1-5. The Apostle Paul gives married couples some spiritual guidance about sex and in verse 5 he says, "Do not deprive each other except perhaps by mutual consent and for a time, so that you may devote yourselves to prayer."

Yep, Paul is talking about a husband and wife fasting sex. I am doing my best not to write every joke currently going through my mind!

But Paul says to refrain *for a time*. A fast doesn't mean a new way of life nor does it entail permanently ridding something from your life. A fast has a beginning and an end. This is different from him calling you to abstain from something—that's not a fast. That's God's conviction!

We all come to a point where we need to take a few moments (or days) to refrain from something that takes up time and space in our lives and instead dedicate that time to God.

I think that one of the most important fasts we can do in our day and age

DAY 13

is a media fast. Unplug your TV for a while. Put down your phone. Turn off your radio. I'll talk more about the noise in our culture tomorrow, but over the next few weeks I want to encourage you to be open to things that God might want you to remove from your life for a time, so that you can focus more on him.

In two days we begin our first media fast. During this fast I encourage you to abstain from watching TV and playing video games. Stay off your smart phones and turn off your computer when you're not at work. Drive with the radio off and avoid filling that time by talking on the phone. Instead, go for a walk. Have a game night with friends or family. Read a book *(although books were the earliest form of media!)*.

Learn how to live with more silence.

BIBLE STUDY

1. Read 1 Corinthians 7:1-5. What does God say about depriving ourselves, even of the godly things?

_____

_____

_____

_____

2. When we do deprive ourselves, what should our focus be?

_____

_____

_____

_____

PERSONAL APPLICATION

1. What are a few things that you could fast to make some more time for God?

_____

_____

_____

_____

CLOSING PRAYER

God help me to fill the void of noise with thoughts of you. Help me to put down my idols of media that have such a grip on my life. Help me to enjoy your presence more. Help me to find satisfaction in friendships, family and fellowship. Amen.

DAY 14

TUNE OUT THE WORLD AND LISTEN

by Brian McMillan, Lead Pastor

SCRIPTURE VERSE

"He says, 'Be still, and know that I am God; I will be exalted among the nations, I will be exalted in the earth.'" Psalm 46:10

DEVOTIONAL

I was recently at a monster truck show with my kids. I have to say, I hated it! I don't like loud. The roar of monster truck engines echoing in the arena was more than I could stand. My son asked me to buy him a hotdog, but I came back with a soda. I just couldn't hear him over the ruckus.

This is modern day life: LOUD. Excessive noise is everywhere. Thanks to technology, we live in a constant din: cellphones, iPods, radio, television, computers and even elevator music. No matter where you go, you hear background noise. We are bombarded with audio stimulation at every turn. And I don't think we can really hear over the volume.

This is not natural.

We need silence. The human brain needs rest, it needs silence. Yet we are so used to constant noise that we don't know how to function without it. Quiet makes us uneasy. We panic and reach for the closest noise-inducing piece of technology to destroy the loathed silence.

There are spiritual consequences to this.

Because of all the clamor, we fail to hear faint sounds. Once, when the radio in my car was broken, I heard the strangest sounds coming from my car. It sounded so unnatural. I brought it to the mechanic and, to my surprise, he said the car was fine. I finally realized I had never driven it without music playing so I had no idea how the car was supposed to sound!

I see the parallel in us as Christians: The Holy Spirit is trying to speak to us, but because there is so much residual noise, we can't hear him.

If an army wants to win a battle, it should destroy its enemy's communications capabilities. If one side cannot receive orders from its commanders, it won't know how to proceed and will likely lose for lack of leadership. Likewise, if we can't hear from God, we will be defeated.

I wonder, do we even know what the Christian life is supposed to *sound* like?

These 40 days are about intentionality, about seeing greater opportunities and taking them. So let's take this opportunity to unplug. Remove your headphones. Turn off your radio. Silence your cellphone. And just listen. In the silence you will hear the voice of God.

BIBLE STUDY

1. Read 1 King 19:9b-13. What was God trying to teach Elijah (and us) through this experience?

_____

_____

_____

2. How did Elijah know that God was in the whisper instead of the other events that unfolded before him?

_____

_____

_____

DAY 14

PERSONAL APPLICATION

1. When was the last time you were intentional about creating silent spaces in your life?

_____

_____

_____

2. What did you gain through that experience?

_____

_____

_____

_____

_____

CLOSING PRAYER

Shut out all the "noise" in your life. Spend the next five minutes in silence listening for the voice of the Lord.

WEEK 3

FOCUS ON GOD'S WORD

DAY 15

OUR DAILY BREAD

by Henry Fuhrman, Executive Pastor of Ministries

SILENCE

Begin your time with two minutes of silence and stillness before God. This will help clear your head of all the distractions of your day and center your thoughts on the Lord.

SCRIPTURE VERSE

"Give us today our daily bread." Matthew 6:11

DEVOTIONAL

At the heart of the prayer Jesus taught us is a simple and profound request: "Give us today our daily bread."

Our daily bread is not something we earn; it is something that is given to us by a gracious God. After all, "He opens his hand and satisfies the desires of every living thing." All that we have comes from the God who provides (Psalm 145:16). This is reminiscent of the daily bread that God gave the Israelites every morning while they were in the wilderness (Exodus 16). Moses instructed the people to "gather only what they need for that day" and to "not store any bread for the morning" (Exodus 16:18-19). The point is clear: We are to rely on God's provision daily and to trust that he will meet our most basic needs.

Requesting bread stands in stark contrast to the extravagant prayers in our culture of consumption. Many of us take responsibility for the things we need and only seek God for the things we want. Jesus challenges us not to ask for luxuries or frivolous desires, but only for our basic needs. In fact, we are told "not to worry about what to eat or what do drink," but to "seek first His kingdom and His righteousness and all these things will be added to us" (Matthew 6:31, 33). In other words, even though food is our most pressing, daily need, our spiritual needs are far greater. "For man does not live by bread alone but by every word that comes from the mouth of God" (Matthew 4:4).

The bread that "comes from the mouth of God" is what we most need to consume. God has given us himself by giving us his Word. Yet too few of us feed regularly on God's Word. A recent study showed that while 80 percent of American Christians believe the Bible is sacred scripture, only 26 percent read it more than four times a week. We have lost sight of a simple truth, to quote John Calvin: "Jesus Christ comes to us clothed in the Scriptures."

We are a people whose most basic need is God himself. We need God to give us our daily bread. More precisely, we need the bread that God has already given us. We need the "bread" that has been revealed—the "bread which has come down from heaven and gives life to the world." (John 6:33) We need him to be the bread that fills our emptiness, day by day.

BIBLE STUDY

1. Read Exodus 16 and list what stands out about God's commands to the Israelites.

_____

_____

_____

2. Read Matthew 6:31-33 and list the "needs" that you worry about most.

_____

_____

_____

DAY 15

PERSONAL APPLICATION

1. Read through and pray the Lord's prayer as found in Matthew 6:9-13.

_____

_____

_____

2. Reflect on how God has provided for your basic needs and thank him.

_____

_____

_____

3. Write down at least one way that you can make reading God's Word a part of your daily routine.

_____

_____

_____

CLOSING PRAYER

"'Our Father in Heaven, hallowed be your name, your kingdom come, your will be done on earth as it is in heaven. _Give us today our daily bread._ And forgive us our debts, as we also have forgiven our debtors. And lead us not into temptation, but deliver us from the evil one.'"

DAY 16

THE INSPIRED WORD OF GOD

by Henry Fuhrman, Executive Pastor of Ministries

SILENCE

Begin your time with two minutes of silence and stillness before God. This will help clear your head of all the distractions of your day and center your thoughts on the Lord.

SCRIPTURE VERSE

"Above all, you must understand that no prophecy of Scripture came about by the prophet's own interpretation. For prophecy never had its origin in the will of man, but men spoke from God as they were *carried along by the Holy Spirit.*" 1 Peter 1:20-21 *(Emphasis added)*

DEVOTIONAL

Peter's statement is astounding! The prophetic writings of the Old Testament were not human in origin, but the prophets, though human, "spoke from God as they were *carried along by the Holy Spirit.*" In other words, God spoke to the prophets and they in turn proclaimed these truths to the people. God revealed his Word and man recorded it.

The words "carried along by the Holy Spirit" are especially significant. The word "carried" that appears here is the same word found in Acts 27:15-17 when the wind "carried" the ship and "drove it along." In Acts 27, experienced sailors were unable to navigate the ship because of the storm. The ship was driven, directed and carried about by the wind. This provides a helpful metaphor for understanding the Spirit's role in scripture: In the same way the wind drove, directed and carried the ship, the Spirit of God drove, directed and carried the human authors of the Bible. In both cases, the sailors and authors were active participants, but in both cases, the wind or the Spirit was at the helm.

This understanding of scripture is known as the Doctrine of Inspiration and it has profound theological and practical implications. It means that even though the Bible is a book, it is unlike any other book in human history. The scriptures themselves are God's very own words for us, inspired by the very same Spirit who indwells all who believe. We cannot approach the Bible like we would a newspaper article, a textbook or historical novel. We should not read the Bible casually or carelessly, since the words of God demand our complete attention. I love what Eugene Peterson says in *Eat This Book*: "If Holy Scripture is to be something other than mere gossip about God, it must be internalized…Words—spoken and listened to, written and read—are intended to do something in us, give health and wholeness, vitality and holiness, wisdom and hope."

God's words are the words we need most to hear, for his words are the only ones that have eternal life (John 6:68). When we read the Bible, we must be intentional about listening to the Holy Spirit in the text and inviting him to plant his truth into the core of our beings. We must approach scripture with hearts eager to be driven, directed and carried by the Spirit.

In the same way the Holy Spirit moved the Bible's writers to record the Word, so does the Holy Spirit aim to move the Bible's readers to respond to the Word.

BIBLE STUDY

1. Read 2 Timothy 3:16 and reflect on the Holy Spirit's role in revealing scripture.

2. Read John 14:26 and describe how the Holy Spirit aids us in understanding God's truth.

_____

_____

_____

PERSONAL APPLICATION

Today, let us not only read but also internalize God's Word and reflect on how God might be leading us each to respond personally. Spend time in silence and in prayer and ask the Holy Spirit to show you how you can personally obey this command from God in your life: "This is what is required of you: Do justice, love mercy, and walk humbly with your God." Micah 6:8

1. How might the Spirit of God be leading you to "do justice"?

_____

_____

_____

2. In what ways might God be leading you to "love mercy"?

_____

_____

_____

3. What practices in your life help you to "walk humbly" with God?

_____

_____

_____

CLOSING PRAYER

Holy Spirit, teach us all things and remind us of everything God has said to us. (John 14:6)

DAY 17

BIBLE READING VS. STUDYING

by John Ulin, Pastor of Discipleship and Spiritual Formation

SCRIPTURE VERSE

"I have hidden your word in my heart that I might not sin against you."
Psalm 119:11

SILENCE

Take two minutes to quietly reflect on this verse.

DEVOTIONAL

I don't know about you, but I was pretty intellectually lazy throughout middle school and most of high school. For example, I really despised doing book reports. Why guess what the author was thinking or presume his intention in writing this book? Reading the words on the pages should've been good enough, in my opinion. (Fortunately, my sister was patient enough to set me straight!)

All of us face the temptation to be intellectually lazy in our approach to the Bible. But if we are, we will miss out on knowing God better. Think about it: Of everything God could have revealed to mankind (he's omniscient, remember), he narrowed it down to what we have in the Bible. That means that every word in every verse in every chapter of every book has a purpose.

2 Timothy 3:16-17 says that scripture is breathed out by God and is profitable for teaching, correction, reproof and training in righteousness so that God's people can be adequately equipped for every good work. Every time

we open the Bible we have the opportunity for spiritual growth. We should not expect significant transformation if we just peruse the Word. It won't happen. However, if we consistently take time to reflect and pray about even one verse, God will use it to grow our faith and godliness.

One of the best ways to study God's Word is to write down your questions and observations as you go through a text. You can ask: *Which words in this verse were different when you read it in another translation? Is a word or portion of this text confusing?* Researching the answers to these questions using commentaries will add a new dimension to your spiritual life and help you transition from *reading* the Bible to *studying* it.

A second way to study God's Word is in community. You can review the scriptures from a Sunday message and study them prior to your life group meeting. Then, during the discussion portion of the meeting, bring it up.

Sure, that's more work than just reading a verse or chapter for the day and moving on to the next item on a to-do list. But you can take a different approach each time you read the Bible. For example, I may read through an entire story or Gospel to appreciate the big picture or the aerial view. And yet sometimes I take a close-up look at one verse so I can admire the beauty in the details.

I pray that as we spend time studying the Word we will recognize the inevitable growth in our understanding of God and, then, willingly devote even more time to study his Word.

BIBLE STUDY/PERSONAL APPLICATION

1. What time each day will you set aside to study the Bible (morning before work, lunch break, as soon as I get home from work, before I go to bed)?

_____

_____

_____

2. Read the Bible with a notebook handy for writing down questions.

DAY 17

3. Read Psalm 119:103-105 in two to three translations (i.e. KJV, NIV, ESV) and write down the words that are different in each.

_____

_____

_____

_____

CLOSING PRAYER

Heavenly Father, I thank you for your Word. Help me see such value in reading and studying the Bible so that I will make the necessary sacrifices in my schedule to do so. Grant me the humility to admit when I don't understand something and the desire to seek the answers in those resources you've made available. Let me hide your Word in my heart so that I grow in godliness, for your name and glory. Amen.

How sweet are your thy words to my taste
Sweeter than honey to my mouth
Thru your precepts I get understanding therefore I hate every false way path

DAY 18

MEDITATE ON GOD'S WORD

by Jean Impert, Ministry Intern

SCRIPTURE VERSE

"Oh how I love your law! It is my meditation all the day." Psalm 119:97

DEVOTIONAL

I'm not on Instagram and I barely (more like never) use Twitter. The hashtag culture has never appealed to me. I like engaging with others and keeping current, but the concept of social media in general—and all its platforms—doesn't appeal to me. There's too much to keep up with and, to borrow a phrase, TMI. *"Hey, I'm eating at this amazing restaurant that you've never been to eating a delicious meal you wish you had!"* There's #mcm, #wcw, #tbt and surely a litany of abbreviations of which I'm completely unaware.

Social media is a reflection of our culture: fast-paced; ever changing; now, now, now! Within a couple hours today's news becomes yesterday's news. Attention spans have dwindled and we communicate via text lingo and abbreviated English. This is just the way it is. smh.

This has infiltrated our thinking as believers. Many of us get caught up in what I call "Catchphrase Christianity." We cling to the latest spiritual trend until the next one comes along. The seasons are short lived and shallow. These trends aren't bad in and of themselves, but they become like everything else: feeding our low attention spans then getting kicked by the wayside when the next trending idea comes along. Nothing sticks. Nothing penetrates. Nothing leaves an indelible impression on our hearts, our minds and our souls.

DAY 18

As Christians, we have strayed from the practice of meditating on the Word of God. When most people think of meditation, they visualize a bald monk sitting on a burlap rug humming a hypnotizing, tantric, repetitive phrase. Although this could be *his* form of meditation, this is not what the Bible means. When you are in a romantic relationship, you are most likely on the phone for hours. When apart, your thoughts are consumed by that person. The smallest thing reminds you of them and brings a smile to your face. This is more what the Bible means by meditation: Your thoughts and emotions are completely overtaken by one singular focus, namely Christ.

We must meditate on the Word in order to immerse ourselves in the reality of our good, gracious and glorious God. Praying, reading our Bibles, going to church or even serving in ministry is not enough. Our minds and our hearts must dwell on the Word.

I love to cook. The best way to get lots of flavor into meat is to marinate it. The process of marinating does two things: It infuses the marinade's flavor into the meat—the longer it sits in the marinade, the more flavor it absorbs; and it breaks down the meat's tough fibers. How unpleasant is it to chew on a rubbery piece of meat?

What if we marinated ourselves in God's Word? He would impart more of himself into us. We would begin to resemble the essence of the Word, Jesus. We would become more receptive to the Holy Spirit and show less resistance to his leading. God's Word has a way of breaking us and shaping us more into the image of Christ. This process, sanctification, is not meant to be pleasant—after all it is breaking down our fleshly desires. But it is necessary. Steep, stew and sit in the Word and let it transform you.

So, what does meditation actually look like? First, it requires stillness. This doesn't necessarily mean quiet or silence, although it can for some. Your mind must be still. Shut out everything—the errands that need to be run, the paper that needs to be finished, the bills that need to be paid, the kids' soccer practice. Be still. Give God your undivided attention.

Secondly, dissect a Scripture. I like doing this word by word or phrase by phrase. You can also do this by breaking down a passage into sections. For example:

"For God so loved the world"
"That He gave His only Son"
"That whoever believes in Him"
"Should not perish"
"But have eternal life"

This is what you call ruminating (thinking carefully and deeply about something) on a Scripture. Ask yourself: *What comes to mind when you read, "For God so loved the world?" Isn't it amazing that God would love the world in all of its darkness and sinful rebellion against him? How has he loved me? From what has that love delivered me? How do I love others?* This is just an example of what you can do with any portion of scripture.

Meditation requires much more attention span than social media. This is your time with the Word, *with God*. Be still. Read. Dissect the passage. Ruminate on it.

BIBLE STUDY

Hebrews 4:12 says, "For the word of God is living and active, sharper than any two-edged sword, piercing to the division of soul and of spirit, of joints and of marrow, and discerning the thoughts and intentions of the heart."

1. According to Hebrews 4:12, what is the Word and what does it discern?

    _____

    _____

    _____

2. What are the other descriptions of the Word from this passage? Does this seem violent and tumultuous or pleasant and peaceful?

    _____

    _____

    _____

DAY 18

PERSONAL APPLICATION

1. About what do you spend the majority of your time thinking?

_____

_____

_____

2. Do you love the Word of God? If so, has this drawn you to meditate more on it? If not, what is holding you back from loving it?

_____

_____

_____

CLOSING PRAYER / MEDITATION CHALLENGE

Spend five minutes meditating on Hebrews 4:12. Tell the Father that you want to love his Word. Don't rush. After this time is up, pray that God opens your mind to his truth and that his Word is made alive in you.

DAY 19

CHOICES THAT CHANGE US: MEMORIZING SCRIPTURE

by Anthony Bonura, Pastor of Congregational Care

SCRIPTURE VERSE

"I have hidden your word in my heart that I might not sin against you."
Psalm 119:11

DEVOTIONAL

If you could do something that had the potential to greatly benefit your life, you would be foolish not to do it. If you knew this choice would impact your spiritual walk, work, personal life, social life and your emotional wellbeing—for a life time—surely you would go for it!

Though I haven't played baseball for years, I still remember the drills. We batted, fielded ground balls and practiced "situational drills" until they were committed to memory. As a result, I instinctively knew what to do in any situation on game day. Forty years later I automatically know what to do if, say I'm playing second base with runners on first and second, nobody out and the batter is bunting. It was ingrained in my memory.

Memorizing scripture has the same result as these drills. Once you've memorized scripture you will find that your reactions are governed by the Word that is hidden in your heart. When you become angry and are about to set into motion some hurtful and destructive behaviors, the scripture from James 1:20 will pop up: "For man's anger does not bring about the righteous life that God desires." The Word of God will influence you and change the direction of a situation.

In his book *Growing Strong in the Seasons of Life,* Chuck Swindoll said,

DAY 19

"I know of no other single practice in the Christian life more rewarding, practically speaking, than memorizing scripture...no other single exercise pays greater spiritual dividends. Your prayer life will be strengthened. Your witnessing will be sharper and more effective. Your attitudes and outlook will begin to change. Your mind will become alert and observant. Your confidence and assurance will be enhanced. Your faith will be solidified."

Memorizing scripture gives you a tool to use when temptation starts to overtake you (1 Corinthians 10:13) or when a loved one needs a word of comfort and encouragement (Psalm 23:4; Psalm 119:76). When you memorize scripture you will find that your emotions are more settled and peaceful because God's Word becomes the influence over your mind and heart. Having scripture established in your memory enables you to know the God of scripture in a deeper and more intimate way.

This practice continues to transform my life. I have seen my own reactions change as I respond with the Word hidden in my heart. I find that words of comfort and wisdom are on my tongue when they are needed most.

Memorization of Bible verses is something we can all do! It can and will change you. Are you ready to join me in memorizing scripture? Are you ready to have your heart and mind changed by God's word?

You can begin by reading and then memorizing one scripture each week this month from the list below:

"Therefore, if anyone is in Christ he is a new creation; the old has gone, the new has come!" 2 Corinthians 5:17

"Even youths grow tired and weary, and young men stumble and fall; but those who hope in the Lord will renew their strength. They will soar on wings like eagles; they will run and not grow weary, they will walk and not be faint." Isaiah 40:30-31

"For I am convinced that neither death nor life, neither angels nor demons, neither the present nor the future, nor any powers, neither height nor depth, nor anything else in all creation, will be able to separate us from the love of God that is in Christ Jesus our Lord." Romans 8:38-39

"The Lord is my light and my salvation—whom shall I fear? The Lord is the stronghold of my life—of whom shall I be afraid?" Psalm 27:1

BIBLE STUDY

Read Deuteronomy 6. Moses tells the Israelites to obey the commands, decrees and laws of the Lord so, "it may be well" with them. Moses explained various ways the Israelites could keep these commands ever before them. These principles can apply to us today.

1. What are some of the benefits of knowing and keeping the decrees of God?

_____

_____

_____

_____

2. What methods did Moses gives to help the Israelites keep the Word of God "ever before" them?

_____

_____

_____

PERSONAL APPLICATION

Memorize today's scripture verse in this devotional.

CLOSING PRAYER

Lord, I thank you that you have given me your Word to guide, teach and strengthen me. I ask that you would help me as I begin to commit your Word to memory.

UNWRAPPING THE GIFT OF THE SABBATH

by Henry Fuhrman, Executive Pastor of Ministries

SILENCE

Begin your time with two minutes of silence and stillness before God. This will help clear your head of all the distractions of your day and center your thoughts on the Lord.

SCRIPTURE VERSE

"Observe the Sabbath day by keeping it holy, as the LORD your God has commanded you." Deuteronomy 5:12

DEVOTIONAL

When it comes to keeping the Sabbath, there is much misunderstanding. For many, keeping the Sabbath means abiding by strict rules and regulations; do not work; do not drive; do not watch TV, etc. For others, this commandment is completely ignored and the "Sabbath" is impossible to distinguish from other days of the week. We allow busyness with work, sports and other activities to prevent us from living in the God-given rhythm of work and rest. In both cases we miss the point of the Sabbath and fail to receive it as the gift God intends.

Sabbath-keeping is not about abstaining from a list of prohibitions and it's so much more than just taking a day off. As Dorothy Bass observes, "Keeping Sabbath is about being recalled to our knowledge of and gratitude for God's activity in creating the world, giving liberty to captives, and overcoming the powers of death." I especially love how Bass draws a connection between keeping Sabbath and expressing gratitude for our freedom. She reminds us that, "in Deuteronomy the commandment to 'observe the Sabbath day' is tied to the experience of a people newly released from bondage. Slaves cannot take a day off; free people can."

Each time we unwrap the gift of the Sabbath we receive our emancipation from slavery. As we detach from our work, we are freed to see God's work. In setting aside time to pray, we are freed to connect with God. As we move away from all we *do* for God, we become free to simply be with God.

When you keep the Sabbath you release yourself to enjoy life and the love of God. And you experience the freedom of doing absolutely nothing, knowing that God still loves you.

BIBLE STUDY

There is a famous story in the Bible about two women who Jesus knew. When Jesus visited their home, one was busy with preparations while the other sat at his feet.

Read Luke 10:38-42 and answer the following questions.

1. Is the world you live in filled with more Mary's or Martha's?

_____

2. In what ways do your daily activities distract you from being with God?

_____

_____

_____

3. How often do you find yourself simply sitting at the feet of Jesus?

_____

_____

_____

DAY 20

PERSONAL APPLICATION

We were created to live in the rhythm of work and rest, not in the non-stop, greed-filled, idolatrous workaholic nature of our fast-paced culture. In order to "keep Sabbath" you will have to swim against the cultural current and create an intentional plan. Tomorrow is Sunday. Be intentional about experiencing Sabbath tomorrow. Find time for quiet, for prayer, and for fun. No work allowed. Disconnect from social media. And, light a candle as a reminder of God's presence. Experience the gift of resting in God and live one day in the freedom that he has given you.

CLOSING PRAYER

Lord, help me set aside all that distracts me from you and reclaim the gift of being with you.

WEEK 4

FOCUS ON GIVING TO GOD

DAY 21

SOLITUDE

by Jonelle Wuttke, Director of Children's Ministries

SCRIPTURE VERSE

"But Jesus often withdrew to lonely places and prayed." Luke 5:16

DEVOTIONAL

Solitude is defined by Webster's dictionary as the "state of being alone." How does that make you feel?

We live in an era where we are never alone. WiFi, 5G networks, social media, FaceTime, Skype and many other apps and technologies connect us to other people, ideas and trends with a swipe of a finger.

But this connectedness can cause a major disconnect in our relationships with families, spouses, children, friends and with God. We experience the "fear of missing out" or FOMO. Ironically, our "connection" actually forms a rift. To truly know and share our hearts, we must silence our minds (and phones!).

Jesus was busy and sought after. As his popularity grew and word about him spread, multitudes of people sought him, whether out of need or curiosity. Daily. Had he so chosen, Jesus' life could have been something like ours: saturated by people's statuses, pictures and news feeds. But he chose a different path.

Three different Scriptures across three of the Gospels mention that Jesus withdrew to private, solitary places (Matthew 14:13, Luke 5:16, John 6:15). Jesus knew that he needed to be alone in order to hear the heart of God, to commune with his Father, to share his heart for the people amongst whom he was walking.

Practicing the discipline of solitude is not punishment. Being sent to our rooms alone as young children to "think of what we've done" may have engendered a negative connotation to solitude. We need to undo that and intentionally attach a positive, refreshing meaning to solitude.

Throughout this study we are expanding our idea of disciplines. Connecting with God goes beyond a daily practice of reading a Bible verse (or two) and praying once or twice. Coming before God daily in a time of silence and solitude can be refreshing and refilling and account for some of the deepest fellowship you will ever experience.

As Richard Foster writes, "Solitude is inner fulfillment. Solitude is more a state of mind and heart than it is a place." Foster redefines solitude for us because withdrawing from our routine allows us to draw closer to God. Times of being "alone" fill our hearts with the knowledge that we are never alone.

BIBLE STUDY

1. Read Matthew 4:1-11 about Jesus in the dessert before his ministry.

2. Read Luke 5:12-16. Jesus was God in human form. Why would he remove himself to a lonely place if crowds were coming from all over to listen to him and be healed?

_____

_____

_____

PERSONAL APPLICATION

1. Foster writes, "What are some steps into solitude? The first thing we can do is to take advantage of the 'little solitudes' that fill our day." List some moments (a morning cup of coffee, the ride home from drop-

DAY 21

ping children at school, the walk to the deli for lunch) when you can be intentional about tuning out the noise and being silent. Take those moments to reorient yourself with God in a quiet and thoughtful way.

2. Plan a time in the next two months when you can have three hours to yourself. Go to a place where no one will bother you (a corner of a local library may be perfect). Seek God, pray, listen, read Scripture, journal your thoughts and goals for the upcoming months. Just *be* and allow God to clear your mind of the worries and race of the day.

CLOSING PRAYER

Dear God, the struggle against solitude is clear in our culture. Please help us embrace solitude. Instill in us a desire for time alone with you, to hear your voice and be steadfast in our oneness with you. May we follow the example of Christ and withdraw for times of solitude with you. In your name, amen.

DAY 22

CLOSE THE DOOR BEHIND YOU

by Henry Fuhrman, Executive Pastor of Ministries

SILENCE

Begin your time with two minutes of silence and stillness before God. This will help clear your head of all the distractions of your day and center your thoughts on the Lord.

SCRIPTURE VERSE

"But when you pray, go into your room, close the door and pray to your Father, who is unseen. Then your Father, who sees what is done in secret, will reward you." Matthew 6:6

DEVOTIONAL

We've all found ourselves in this situation: Your boss calls you into his or her office and says, "Close the door behind you." Those five words cause you to brace yourself for what is about to come. Whether good or bad, this will certainly be an important conversation. No one else was invited. No one else will hear what is said. The next few moments belong to the two of you alone.

Jesus warns us that we are not to pray "as the hypocrites…who love to pray standing in the synagogues and on the street corners to be seen by others" (Matthew 6:5). Jesus is essentially telling us: "When you talk to God, close the door behind you." We should find a quiet space, a secret place where we can be alone with God. We are to shut out everything and everyone and speak with him alone. No one else should be invited. No else needs to hear what will be said. This moment of prayer belongs exclusively to you and God.

DAY 22

God wants us to hear only his voice. He knows the other voices that form our identity and shape our behavior and he knows that unless we shut the door on everyone else, we might end up listening to the other voices instead. I have found what Henri Nouwen said to be true: "The real 'work' of prayer is to become silent and listen to the voice that says good things about me…To gently push aside and silence the many voices that question my goodness and to trust that I will hear the voice of blessing—that demands real effort."

Also, God wants us to shut the door so he can hear from us, and only us. With the door shut, our words to him won't be influenced by what others may have to say. Closing the door behind us is an invitation to be fully ourselves with God. God invites us: "Close the door and be honest with me. Be angry with me. Admit your doubts to me. Worship me."

The great preacher Gardner Taylor assures us that indeed, "There are days when we can bring before God…laughter of joy and gratitude. There will be other days when we can only muster a bitter, angry complaint. Be confident that God will accept whatever we lift up before him, and he will make it serve his purpose and our good."

By closing the door behind us when we talk with God, we create space for God to deal truthfully with us and for us to speak honestly with God. In so doing, we can experience prayer as it was always designed to be: a personal, intimate activity that unlocks the door to God, and to ourselves.

BIBLE STUDY

1. Read Matthew 6 and consider how the "religious people" in Jesus' day prayed as compared to the way He calls His disciples to pray.

2. Jesus is saying that there is a "reward" for what is done in secret. Why do you think this is?

_____

_____

_____

PERSONAL APPLICATION

For your assignment today, find a private space to pray. This could be in your house, in your car, in your office, wherever you can be alone. Find that private place. Walk into the room and close the door behind you. Spend 15 minutes with the door closed in honest conversation and prayer to God. Listen to God. Tell God what's on your mind and heart. Listen, and then speak.

CLOSING PRAYER

"Search me, O God, and know my heart. Test me, and know my anxious thoughts. See if there is any hurtful way in me, and lead me into the everlasting way." (Psalm 139:23-24)

DAY 23

GIVING IN SECRET

by Steff Eggers, Director of Youth

SCRIPTURE VERSE

"But when you give to someone in need, don't let your left hand know what your right hand is doing. Give your gifts in private, and your Father, who sees everything, will reward you." Matthew 6:3-4

DEVOTIONAL

Modern culture is consumed with "putting it all out there." We post details of every aspect of our lives: what we eat, the clothes we wear, where we are, who we are with and what an awesome time we are having.

It's as if we are starved for attention—we post something on social media and then anxiously wait for people to "like" our posts and comment on them. We crave public affirmation and legitimization in our lives.

It's easy to fall victim to this mind-set in our spiritual walk as well, publicizing what we do (prayer, fasting, revelation from the Word. While we should strive to be a follower of Christ, we should not broadcast it. How much time we spend praying or fasting is for the audience of our Heavenly Father who sees us and is proud of us. This is obviously in stark contrast to what is done in today's culture.

In Matthew 6:16-18, Jesus says, "When you fast, do not look somber as the hypocrites do, for they disfigure their faces to show others they are fasting. Truly I tell you, they have received their reward in full. But when you fast, put oil on your head and wash your face, so that it will not be obvious to others that you are fasting, but only to your Father, who is unseen;

and your Father, who sees what is done in secret, will reward you." Jesus was referring to the religious leaders at the time that wanted to be seen as "holy." He taught that the essence of prayer and fasting is private communication with God, not an opportunity to publicly display how spiritual one is. While corporate prayer and fasting is important, Jesus notes here that those who boast of their individual spiritual lives are seeking an audience of humans, not God.

It's okay to let people know that you read your Bible, pray, fast, etc. But Jesus wants the focus to be on him and not on us. So if someone asks you for prayer, pray for them! If you read something in your devotional time and feel to share it with someone, go for it! Just examine your heart and your motives before you do so.

BIBLE STUDY

1. Reread the passage from Matthew 6:3-4. Think about what that really means and what it looks like in action. What are some ways you can give in private?

_____

_____

_____

2. Why do you think Jesus talks so much about doing things for others and praying in private? Why is it important in our walk with Christ to keep our prayer time private?

_____

_____

_____

_____

DAY 23

3. Read Matthew 6:9-13. What do you take away from the simplicity of the prayer Jesus instructs us to pray? What stands out to you in these verses?

_____

_____

_____

_____

_____

CLOSING PRAYER

God, thank you for the gift of prayer. I ask that you would deepen my walk with you. Help me to truly seek you in all I do, and help me to stay humble. I give you the glory for all things in my life! Keep my eyes on you and you alone. Amen.

WEEK 5

FOCUS ON ONE ANOTHER

DAY 24

TAKING CARE OF WHAT IS GOD'S

by Troy Johnson, Executive Director of Operations

SCRIPTURE VERSE

"Every good and perfect gift is from above, coming down from the Father of the heavenly lights, who does not change like shifting shadows." James 1:17

DEVOTIONAL

Anyone who has spent time with a 2 year old quickly realizes that toddlers have a very different take on ownership than adults do. If a child can see it, touch it, take it or even just point at it, he assumes, "It's mine!" It doesn't matter what the item is, who it really belongs to or how valuable or dangerous it is—it's *his!*

Now let us zoom out from this idea. We, as hard working grown-ups, strive to earn a living so we can feed and dress ourselves and live in a warm home. We work harder so we can afford things that improve our quality of life, productivity and fun. We view these belongings as ours. After all, we earned them.

But, suppose that God views us as we view 2 year olds: He loves us and wants us to have his gifts, but he is also probably disappointed to watch us carry on like our possessions are actually our own. In James 1:17, he says that every good thing we have comes from him. So, at the end of the day, everything that I think is "mine" actually belongs to him. I am merely taking care of it while it is in my care.

This is called stewardship—taking care of something that belongs to someone else. In today's reading, Jesus tells us a parable about servants who are each tasked to steward a portion of the master's wealth.

Take a moment to read Matthew 25:14-28. The message is unmistakable: God wants us to multiply his property through our wise use of his gifts. So if your gift is trade skills, use them to help someone who needs home or car repairs. If you have free time, reach out to someone who could use a companion. If you have a large vehicle, use it help someone move. These are just a few examples of stewardship and about how good stewardship can multiply God's gifts to us including our time, talent and yes, treasure.

What about money? We need it and we work hard to earn it. It sure feels like ours. So how can it be God's? The servants in today's reading worked hard, yet what they received was ultimately granted to them by the master. They were rewarded differently according to their labor. Children may work hard to do their chores, but the payment or reward is decided upon by their parents. Likewise, we work and so we receive our paychecks. But the amount is based on our arrangement with the employer. *If we zoom out from the situation, we understand that God, our provider, is behind all this.*

Lastly, the possessions we care for in this life will remain here after we die. Jesus teaches us to focus on the eternal. In his Sermon on the Mount, he tells us that treasure stored up on earth can be destroyed, but that if we use our gifts and resources to do God's work we will store up spiritual treasures in heaven where we will forever benefit from them (Matthew 6:19-21).

No matter how much we cling to his gifts here on earth, they will one day be taken from our hands. We must shift our mindset from ownership to stewardship. Being a good steward means multiplying God's gifts through sharing them. If we do this now, in heaven we will be like a 2 year old happily opening up eternal gifts from the Lord. And hopefully we will hear him echo the words in today's reading: "Good and faithful servant."

BIBLE STUDY

Read Matthew 25:14-28. Jesus is driving home a strong point: We must *use* his gifts and not hoard them for safe keeping. Gifts can be many different things. They can be objects, skills and aptitudes, opportunities, money and relationships just to name a few.

DAY 24

1. According to the master in Jesus' parable, how do we increase our responsibility?

_____

_____

_____

_____

2. The third servant made a very safe decision. Why was the master upset about this?

_____

_____

_____

_____

PERSONAL APPLICATION

1. What are some significant gifts that God has given to you?

_____

_____

_____

2. In what ways can these gifts be used to grow God's kingdom here on earth?

_____

_____

_____

3. In what ways do these gifts bring you joy?

_____

_____

_____

CLOSING PRAYER

Take a moment to reflect on God's gifts to you.

Dear Lord, thank you for all that you have given me. Help me recognize that while I work hard and earn money, that it ultimately comes from you. Open my eyes to see your zoomed-out view of the world and of my life. May I always be aware that you provide all that I need.

DAY 25

GIVING AS WORSHIP

by Troy Johnson, Executive Director of Operations

SCRIPTURE VERSE

"Each man should give what he has decided in his heart to give, not reluctantly or under compulsion, for God loves a cheerful giver." 2 Corinthians 9:7

DEVOTIONAL

Can you recall an occasion when you had a gift for someone and you were so excited to give it to them? It was perfect for the person receiving it, had value and was a reflection of you. Maybe you even wanted to give it early. Do you remember the thrilled reaction of the recipient? Here's another scenario. Has anyone done something for you, as a favor maybe, for which you were so grateful that you were deeply compelled to give them something to demonstrate your appreciation. We can have so much joy when we give and share of ourselves.

The Bible is full of examples of people giving of their time and resources as a way to thank God. They did it not because they were commanded to, but out of an sense of gratitude. Abram (Abraham) was so grateful to God for a military victory that he gave one tenth of his gain to God (Genesis 14:20). Later, God established a sacrifice called the Peace Offering (Leviticus 3), which was purely a sacrifice of thanksgiving. Both King David and Solomon are recorded as making peace offerings after significant events. What set apart the Peace Offering was that most of the meat was not burnt as in other offerings, but it was eaten. In many ways, the Peace Offering was an act of celebration.

In the New Testament, Paul speaks about giving and devotes much of 2 Corinthians to the topic. He thanks the Corinthian church for its donation but it equally thrilled by its happiness and eagerness to send it—eager to the point that verse 8:4 said the church was "begging" to support Paul's work of growing the church. This offering was an outpouring of the church's gratitude because Paul had shared the good news of Jesus with them.

Now, back to that gift that you were so excited to give. Your excitement likely had more to do with what the recipient meant to you than the gift itself. So it is with our gifts to God. Giving as a continuation of your worship makes your offering to the church so much bigger. It spiritually joins you with the other "voices" in worship to create a place where God is glorified, the gospel is proclaimed and lives are forever changed.

Just as the Corinthian church recognized the significance of Paul's ministry, we hope that you recognize that God is moving here at CenterPoint Church. We hope that you are excited to worship with your offering knowing that everything you love about CenterPoint is made possible because of your financial worship. You, as a fellow worshiper, are a significant piece in the fabric of this ministry. It simply cannot exist without your contribution.

May God inspire us to worship through giving.

BIBLE STUDY

1. Read 2 Corinthians 8:1-9. What is the spirit behind the church's giving? For what reason do you think the church made its offering?

_____

_____

_____

_____

_____

_____

DAY 25

2. Describe the significance of Jesus becoming poor so that we might become rich.

_____

_____

_____

_____

PERSONAL APPLICATION

1. When you give, pause to consider the graciousness of God and give thanks for what he has done.

2. What can you do to make giving feel like an extension of worship? *(Tip: Even if you give online during the week, take a moment during the collection to offer up your gift as worship to Him.)*

_____

_____

_____

_____

CLOSING PRAYER

Lord, thank you for your son and for his sacrifice for which I will inherit a place in your kingdom. Never let me forget this, and may my offerings of praise and sacrifice be pleasing to you. Show me how to see my offerings as worship to you. Remind me that as I give and as I yield my finances to you, you are glorified in my life. Ignite in me the joy of Abraham, David and Solomon who celebrated your greatness through their offerings.

DAY 26

GIVING AS A DISCIPLINE

by Troy Johnson, Executive Director of Operations

SCRIPTURE VERSE

"They gave as much as they were able, and even beyond their ability. Entirely on their own." 2 Corinthians 8:3

DEVOTIONAL

The past two days we examined what it means to be a steward of God's gifts. Yesterday we reflected on the significance of worshiping God through financial giving. Now you may be wondering, "Okay, so how much should I give?" Great question! I have certainly asked myself the same thing along with other faith related questions. And as with any spiritual question we need to see what the Bible says.

Let's start by looking at the Old Testament. God ordained tithes, or percentages of giving, at different times for the Israelites. These were to be acts of worship and repentance that allowed for the provision of the temple workers and the needy. This ensured that the Israelites had a healthy dependence on him.

The New Testament answer to this question is, "It depends!" The truth is, the amount you give is between you and God. Some can give more, some can give less. In 2 Corinthians 8:11-14, Paul exhorts, give "according to your means." God does not call us to give the same monetary amount. However, he asks us to sacrifice and to be dependent on him. He also asks us to be obedient to him (2 Corinthians 9:13).

So what amount makes you dependent and causes you to look to him as a provider? You must prayerfully consider this question to arrive at the answer. This is less about a legalistic percentage and more about your heart. Remember yesterday's scripture verse? It is about our eagerness to give.

At CenterPoint Church, we offer practical guidelines that grow with you on your journey of faith:

1. A great way to transition from not giving at all is to make an easy donation. Simply look in your wallet on Sunday and pull out a bill for the offering basket. This is a great way to mark your commitment and a perfect place to begin your giving habit.

2. The next step is to move from an easy gift to intentional giving. This is a routine, more significant amount such as 2 to 8 percent of your salary, or a monthly or weekly gift of a set amount. This category represents a prayerfully considered amount that you intentionally set aside to give back to God. Giving in this way becomes a spiritual discipline as you focus on God's will for your finances.

3. The third suggestion is to move toward giving 10 percent. This is often seen as the gold standard for giving among Christians. I encourage you to do more research about giving a tenth and pray about giving this percentage.

4. Finally, you may be called to be a generous giver. This is a person or family that understands that generosity is one of their *spiritual gifts* (Romans 12:8). Generous givers freely give far more than 10 percent to the church, missionaries and people in need.

So how much *should* you give? This is not a question you can probably answer today. As you are sharpening your focus through this devotional, ask God to give you guidance in your finances to determine the right amount. You may be challenged and convicted that your offering does not match up with what you know God is asking of you.

The goal of this discipline is not to determine how little you can get away with giving, but how much you can worshipfully give. Regardless of how much you give, know that gifts of any amount to CenterPoint Church are carefully used to best serve God's kingdom here on Long Island and around the world.

BIBLE STUDY

1. Read 2 Corinthians 9:6-15. What stands out to you in verses 6 and 7?

_____

_____

2. According to verses 13-15, God is glorified by both sharing the gospel and sharing through generosity. How is this true in today's church?

_____

_____

_____

PERSONAL APPLICATION

1. How will you seek and find the answer to the question, "How much?"

_____

_____

2. How does thinking about giving as a spiritual discipline affect your giving attitude?

_____

_____

CLOSING PRAYER

Dear Lord, it costs so much to live here and I feel financially strapped already. Show me how to depend on you. Show me how to give obediently to your will. Let your will be at work in my finances. Help me to be a cheerful giver. Show me how much to give during this chapter of my life. Lord, I love you and I thank you for all you have provided. Amen.

DAY 27

PEOPLE OF LOVE

by Jonathan Parisi, Ministry Intern

SCRIPTURE VERSE

"Love is patient, love is kind. It does not envy, it does not boast, it is not proud. It does not dishonor others, it is not self-seeking, it is not easily angered, it keeps no record of wrongs." 1 Corinthians 13:4-5

DEVOTIONAL

In his earthly ministry Jesus called us to be people of love. When asked for the greatest commandment he responded, "Love the Lord your God with all your heart and with all your soul and with all your mind. This is the first and greatest commandment. And the second is like it: Love your neighbor as yourself." Love should be present in all of our relationships—with God, friend, family or foe. Jesus was asked for the greatest commandment, yet he gave the second greatest anyway: "Love your neighbor as yourself." Neighbor in this sense is an all-inclusive term: Jesus wants us to love everybody.

He could have left it at "love your neighbor," but he didn't. He added "as yourself." People are naturally selfish and in this command, God is calling us to a selfless, self-sacrificing love for everyone we know. Love is to be filled with grace.

To love as Christ would have us love we must rely on him, our ultimate example of love. Love comes from God because God is love and he performed the ultimate act of love by giving us his son. This is our motivation to love others.

Love is a command and a choice, you will surely not always feel like loving someone in a given moment but remember that Christ loved us even though we never deserved it (Romans 5:6-8). For actions without love are meaningless but true love will always produce action (1 John 3:17-18).

BIBLE STUDY

1. Read 1 Corinthians 13:1-7. Meditate on verses 1-3. What is Paul saying about our actions? Do the motivations of our heart matter just as much as the actions themselves? Why or why not?

_____

_____

_____

_____

_____

2. Now reread verses 4-7. This is an exhaustive list describing what love ought to be. Look over these characteristics of love and examine your life. List each characteristic of love as either a personal strength or weakness. Think deeply about why you think each one is either a strength or a weakness.

_____

_____

_____

_____

_____

PERSONAL APPLICATION

1. Write down the ways you serve others at home, in the workplace, or in church and think about your motivations behind each action. Are

you seeking to help others or are you just seeking God's favor through your actions? Do you feel slighted if you don't receive credit for your actions?

_____

_____

_____

_____

2. Think about the people in your life that you say you love. Do you treat them with the kind of love Paul describes in verses 4-7? Write down some ways you want to be intentional about loving others better.

_____

_____

_____

_____

CLOSING PRAYER

As you close in prayer ask God to give you a pure heart so that you will be motivated to love others by his love for you. Ask for a desire for more of him in your life, and for grace in discipline and prudence as you seek after him. "Create in me a pure heart, O God, and renew a steadfast spirit within me." (Psalm 51:10)

PEOPLE OF LOVE: IN THE CHURCH

by Henry Fuhrman, Executive Pastor of Ministries

SILENCE

Begin your time with two minutes of silence and stillness before God. This will help clear your head of all the distractions of your day and center your thoughts on the Lord.

SCRIPTURE VERSE

"By this everyone will know that you are my disciples, if you love one another." John 13:35

DEVOTIONAL

All of us have had to wrestle with major questions, issues, problems and pain in our lives. And despite popular teaching to the contrary, becoming a Christian does not exempt one from experiencing the difficulties of life. In fact, Jesus emphasizes that faithfully following him will lead us on a road marked by pain and suffering (Matthew 16:24). Fortunately we aren't on this path alone. Jesus not only assures us that he "is with us always" (Matthew 28:20), but he surrounds us with others who, like us, are mere sinners confessing our need of a Savior. This gathering of misfits and rebels is what we call "the Church," the family of God that he is drawing together from around the world.

The Church should be a safe place for those searching for answers in the midst of pain and confusion. It should be a powerful place where the Gospel intersects with "real life" and personal experiences come face to face with hope, love and redemption. As people of God, we should strive to experience not just a change of mind or behavior, but a change of heart so that the Lord can prepare us ordinary people to offer love and compassion to each other in his name. We should be known as a people of love (John 13:35) who carry one another's burdens (Galatians 6:2) and mourn and rejoice with one another (Romans 12:15).

God is love and his people are to be known by his love (1 John 4:8). The Father has loved us and commanded us to love with that same gracious intensity. The early church was known for its love. In the 3rd Century, Tertullian wrote that the Christians' actions of love were so noble that even the pagan world said in astonishment, "See how they love one another." In the following quote, the 2nd Century philosopher Aristides describes the Christian community:

> *They walk in all humility and kindness, and falsehood is not found among them, and they love one another. They despise not the widow, and grieve not the orphan. He that has distributes liberally to him that has not. If they see a stranger, they bring him under their roof, and rejoice over him as if he were their own brother: for they call themselves brethren, not after the flesh, but after the Spirit of God; but when one of their poor passes away from the world, and any of them see him, he provides for his burial according to his ability; and if they hear that any of their number is imprisoned or oppressed for the name of their Messiah, all of them provide for his needs. ... And if there is among them a man that is needy and poor, and they have not an abundance of necessaries, they fast two or three days that they may supply the needy with their necessary food.*

It is amazing that the early Christians were known as people who didn't just talk about love, but people who showed love to one another. If these same words cannot describe the Church today, I think we have to wonder why.

BIBLE STUDY

1. Read John 13:34-35 and John 15:12, and take note of what Jesus commands here.

_____

_____

2.   Read 1 John 4:7-10 and reflect on the Biblical definition of love.

_____

_____

_____

PERSONAL APPLICATION

1.   How well do you think the people in the church love one another?

_____

_____

_____

2.   How well do you obey Jesus' command to "love one another" in the church?

_____

_____

_____

3.   Write down one way you can show the love of Christ to one person at CenterPoint.

_____

_____

_____

CLOSING PRAYER

Dear God, since you have so loved us, help us, show us, and lead us to love one another.

DAY 29

PEOPLE OF LOVE: SERVICE

by Nachbi Lacossiere, Director of College and Career Ministries

SCRIPTURE VERSE

"Dear friends, let us love one another, for love comes from God. Everyone who loves has been born of God and knows God. Whoever does not love does not know God, because God is love." 1 John 4:7-8

DEVOTIONAL

The word "service" usually conjures up feelings of strenuous activity, long days, putting others' needs before your own and no real me time. Many of us have been scarred by this perspective of serving and it has caused us to step back and conclude, "serving isn't for me."

But whether it feels like service or not, we all serve someone or something. The difference is that when service is driven by love it doesn't have those negative connotations. For example, I love my family and this love comes easy regardless of the circumstances. Because I've been through so much with them—laughing and crying together, good and bad days—serving my family comes naturally. It doesn't feel like the above view of service.

Psalm 82:3 says, "Defend the weak and the fatherless; uphold the cause of the poor and the oppressed." When God transforms our hearts we begin to see the world the way he sees it and we begin to care for the same things he does. The deep compassion God has for the fatherless, the poor and the oppressed becomes a part of us. We uphold the cause of those in need. We pray for and help the afflicted. We bring the good news to desolate places. These actions are woven into our fabric as God's love transforms us into people of love. Suddenly service becomes a way of life rather than a task.

The church is called to be intentional in serving our respective communities. This can be done through food pantries, service projects, volunteering at church, missions trips, building relationships with those who may feel forgotten and in other ways you feel God is leading you.

When you enter into the realm of service, take it one step at a time. It may seem intimidating at first, but seek the hand of God in each task and watch him perform miracles in your midst.

BIBLE STUDY

"If you pour yourself out for the hungry and satisfy the desire of the afflicted, then shall your light rise in the darkness and your gloom be as the noonday." Isaiah 58:10

1. Am I someone who pours myself out for the hungry and the afflicted?

_____

_____

_____

_____

2. In what ways can I serve so that my light rises in the darkness around me?

_____

_____

_____

_____

DAY 29

PERSONAL APPLICATION

1. Is there anyone that you love to serve, that serving them feels more like love and less like service? Why is that?

_____

_____

_____

_____

2. Are you making space in your life to love God so you can truly serve others?

_____

_____

_____

_____

CLOSING PRAYER

Lord Jesus, help me to create space to truly know you and love you. Consume me with your never-ending love and allow me to love and serve the world around me.

DAY 30

PEOPLE OF LOVE: MISSIONAL

by Brian McMillan, Lead Pastor

SCRIPTURE VERSE

"Everyone who calls on the name of the Lord will be saved." Romans 10:13

DEVOTIONAL

Over the last three days, we spoke about God's call for us to love people. Love is the defining attribute of God himself and, therefore, of us as his followers. We should do everything out of love including how we show people that God loves them.

When I was growing up, I was taught about the importance of evangelism. Evangelism is the act of sharing the salvation of Jesus to people who don't know him. In the church, we were given tools to do this and took courses in apologetics so we could explain how our faith is grounded in reason. Then we were sent out to tell people about Jesus. We went to the boardwalk or to the mall. We used a spiritual survey as an ice breaker, shared the gospel and, when the conversation ended, went on to the next person.

Occasionally, someone took a step of faith. Even fewer joined the church. To say that all this effort didn't bear much fruit would be an understatement. People don't trust strangers, especially strangers talking about God! Long Islanders would rather get financial advice from a homeless person than listen to a well-meaning random Christian tell them about Jesus.

I'm not knocking street evangelism. I think some are called to it. But I don't think that's what Jesus meant when he gave the Great Commission: "All authority in heaven and on earth has been given to me. Therefore go and

DAY 30

make disciples of all nations, baptizing them in the name of the Father and of the Son and of the Holy Spirit, and teaching them to obey everything I have commanded you." (Matthew 28:18-20)

Our calling is higher than simply sharing our faith with strangers and walking away. The New Testament pattern requires sharing *our lives* with those estranged from God. Being missional means being truly invested in people's lives so that they see your faith as you live it, in word and deed. It's befriending someone. It's truly caring about someone's joy, pain, dreams, struggles and desires. Jesus befriended sinners. Paul went to foreign towns and lived among those far from God.

We must have real relationships with those who don't know Christ if we want to walk as people of love. We live in a hurting world: People need to experience the love and grace of Jesus and understand that God has a plan for them. They need to know what it really means to follow Jesus. But for that to happen, they need to *know you!* Not from a distance, but up close. They need to be a part of your life.

We must practice the spiritual disciplines of hospitably and evangelism. To open our lives, homes and time. Then as we share about salvation in Jesus, people will know that he exists in us!

BIBLE STUDY

1. Read Romans 10:11-15. Who is Paul expecting to share this news?

_____

_____

2. As you read the Great Commission in Matthew 28:18-20, what do you think it means to "make disciples" and what responsibilities fall on us in this process?

_____

_____

_____

PERSONAL APPLICATION

1. What are the circles in your life that have nothing to do with church?

_____

_____

_____

_____

2. When people look at your life, do you think they see Jesus at work in you?

_____

_____

_____

_____

3. Write the names of three to five people you know who are far from God. Spend time praying for them every day.

_____

_____

_____

CLOSING PRAYER

Heavenly father, give me a heart for those that are far from you. Help me to be more open so that I can share your good news through how I live. God, allow my home to be a place of hospitality, a place people can come and feel your love. Give me the courage to share the story you have written on my heart and the good news I have found in you. Amen.

DAY 31

PRIORITIZATION

by Troy Johnson, Executive Director of Operations

SCRIPTURE VERSE

"One hand full of rest is better than two fists full of labor and striving after wind." Ecclesiastes 4:4

DEVOTIONAL

Many people are overworked, stressed out and maintain busy lifestyles. Certainly we can expect busy seasons in our lives (college, raising young children, caring for someone who is sick), but for some this may describe your life year after year. If it does, recognize that you can make choices that, when aligned with your priorities, can give you more room to breathe. Otherwise you pay a price spiritually, physically and in your relationships.

Pastor Andy Stanley discussed this in his book *Take it to the Limit*. He acknowledges the busy lifestyle then he shifts attention to what holds it together: the margin. Margin is the space between dance class and soccer. Between waking up and going to chemistry class. Between one obligation and the next. Margin is our buffer from non-stop action. It's our time for loved ones. It allows us to deal with emergencies or help others on our way. It's our time for God. Chances are you are fitting this reading into the margin of your day.

Consider this page. It too has margins. The space between the edge of the page and the text gives you an area to write your reflections. Your eyes have an easier time reading due to this white space. And it makes the page look nicer, more breathable. Like pages, our lives need margins.

Now what if I had more to say but the margins of this page would not allow me to write it? Should I reduce the margins in order to pack in all of my points? I could also eliminate paragraph breaks and keep on writing. I could even make the font smaller! Obviously, all of this would make the page look crammed, be difficult to read and, in the end, you probably wouldn't even be able to pick out my main point. I need to prioritize what I write.

To prevent the margins in our lives from disappearing, they need to be *defined* and *defended*. When you prioritize, and then make decisions based on those priorities, you have to make sacrifices elsewhere. Adding something else that doesn't fit into your priorities means less margin time. If you add something, you have to cut back on other things whether sleep, devotional time, life group or family time. Be mindful to defend the space on your page so you can be fully available for your priorities!

Prioritizing keeps you focused on what is most important: God, family/relationships and career/ministry. Prioritizing means *you may even need to say no to something really worthwhile!*

Setting boundaries to make room for your priorities is an essential discipline. If you don't you will be unable to apply what you have read during the last 34 days! You need to know your limits and be intentional about what fits inside them. Take control of your priorities so that you commune with God instead of giving him your leftover time.

BIBLE STUDY

Read Hebrews 11:39-12:3. Hebrews 11 is about heroes of faith and what they gave up for the sake of God's kingdom. The author exhorts us to set aside our distractions to focus on the importance of God's work in our lives.

1.   What are we supposed to throw off or lay aside? Why?

_____

_____

_____

2. How can remembering Jesus' sacrifice help us in our "race?"

_____

_____

_____

PERSONAL APPLICATION

1. What would you give up if it meant you could give more attention to spiritual disciplines?

_____

_____

_____

2. What can you leave unfinished or imperfect so you can connect more with God and others?

_____

_____

_____

CLOSING PRAYER

Dear Lord, help me find the margins in my day for you—time to pray, time to consider your greatness and time to love my brothers and sisters. Show me where I need to say "no" or "not now" to preserve the boundaries in my life. Show me what to cut or to push further down the list so that my priorities are in an order that is pleasing to you and bearable for me. Thank you also Lord for giving me strength and endurance to get through tough seasons when margins are squeezed. Amen.

DAY 32

ACCOUNTABILITY

by John Ulin, Pastor of Discipleship and Spiritual Formation

SCRIPTURE VERSE

"Confess your sins to each other and pray for each other so that you may be healed." James 5:16

SILENCE

Take two minutes to quietly reflect on this verse.

DEVOTIONAL

I love snorkeling. It may sound strange, but when I snorkel I'm in a state of worship—there is such beauty underwater and our God is responsible for all of it. I once had the opportunity to do a group snorkeling tour in the Caribbean. One of the major advantages of going with a group is that the combined vision of all of the divers compensates for the limitations of our individual goggles. So if I miss something a fellow snorkeler taps my arm and points it out to me (and vice versa). On this trip, we had a wonderful experience because we helped each other see more than we would have individually. I believe this same principle applies to our spiritual lives.

We all have blind spots in life. Our limited perspectives as finite beings make it impossible to see the whole picture all of the time. And this is why we need friends who have the courage (and our permission) to help us see something we may be missing.

One of my struggles is that I judge situations too quickly. Fortunately, I have a wonderful friend named Gary who for the past few years points this out whenever he catches me acting like I am omniscient. "We don't have all the information," is one of his famous lines. The Word says, "Faithful are the wounds of a friend" (Proverbs 27:6). I haven't always received his counsel with a smile—"iron sharpening iron" creates a lot of friction—but I am confident that I have lived in a more Christ-like manner because someone is watching out for my blind spots (Psalm 32:3-5). I have someone who desires for me to be so Christ-like that he'll lovingly point out my inconsistencies. Because of his willingness to pray for me and speak the truth to me in grace I have avoided plenty of mistakes that would have dishonored God.

One of the main reasons we love small groups so much at CenterPoint is because they create an environment for us to develop deep friendships with other Christians that will spread Christ's likeness in each other. These are relationships in which we understand that though we are all sinners saved by grace, we "spur one another on toward love and good deeds" (Hebrews 10:24-25).

My prayer is that each of us would have a believer in our lives that we would allow to ask us the tough questions, so that we can walk in a manner worthy of the Lord to please Him in all respects. My challenge is that you would find someone to help look out for your blind spots (James 5:16).

SUGGESTIONS FOR ACCOUNTABILITY

*   Men meet with men; women meet with women.

*   Meet regularly. This doesn't have to be every week, but shouldn't be whenever you feel like it either.

*   Sample questions:

    1. What struggles are hurting your relationship with God?

    2. Are you putting into practice what you have learned from God's Word?

    3. Are you growing in your love for others (in words and deeds)?

    4. Is there anyone you need to ask for forgiveness?

5. Are you praying for and taking time to share the Gospel with co-workers, neighbors, friends, family members and strangers?

• Keep it private.

BIBLE STUDY

1. Read James 5:16. If we are all sinners, why do you think it is so difficult for many Christians to share their struggles with other Christians?

_____

_____

_____

_____

2. How can James tell everyone to confess their sins and pray and then call those people who do so "righteous?"

_____

_____

_____

_____

PERSONAL APPLICATION

1. Write down the names of two Christian friends who you consider to be spiritually mature.

_____

_____

_____

2. Within the next two days, ask one of them if they would be willing to ask you the above questions once a month for a year. If he or she cannot, ask the other.

_____

_____

_____

CLOSING PRAYER

Jesus, I thank you for taking away all of my sin. Please give me the courage to share my struggles with the mature Christians you've placed in my life so that I can grow in my faith. Give me the humility to listen to their counsel and implement the truths in your Word. In Jesus' name I pray, amen.

DAY 33

A LIFE OF WORSHIP

by Shana Carroll, Director of Worship

SCRIPTURE VERSE

"Therefore, I urge you, brothers and sisters, in view of God's mercy, to offer your bodies as a living sacrifice, holy and pleasing to God—this is your true and proper worship." Romans 12:1

DEVOTIONAL

In Christian circles, the word worship takes on different meanings to different people. To some it means singing at church. For others it's the music on Christian radio. Many of us set apart just Sunday for "worship" and go about our routine the others days of the week. But friends, it is more than just Sunday or radio music. Worship is the daily adoration, devotion, reverence, exaltation and awe of God in every area of our lives.

In the 11 chapters preceding the verse above, Paul writes about the gospel, Christ's love and God's grace. Then in the beginning of chapter 12, Paul sums up the previous chapters saying that in light of understanding salvation, love and grace, it is only logical that we worship with everything we are and offer our bodies as a living sacrifice.

We can worship at all times: while at our jobs, schools, with our families, even while grocery shopping! When we shift our focus from worship being something we do one day a week to it being a part of our entire existence, our eyes are opened to so many opportunities to bring glory to God.

As a mostly stay-at-home mom, I struggle with feeling like many of my daily tasks are mundane and monotonous: Feed the kids, clean up after

DAY 33

them, repeat all day, then collapse into sleep. Yet when I read this passage in Romans, I'm reminded of my calling—to live a life of worship. I challenge myself and ask Jesus for eyes to see that even folding laundry can be done unto God. I thank Him for clean clothes, for my washer and dryer, for hands that work.

At our jobs, we can praise God for our employment, pray for our coworkers and honor Him by being honest in all that we do. We can worship with our finances, through our offerings and by giving freely to those in need. Our relationships can glorify God when we love and care for one another.

It's interesting that Paul tells us to "offer our bodies." This requires action. Worship doesn't depend on a feeling. It's a choice, a decision to give everything thing we are everyday to God who is pleased when we do so.

BIBLE STUDY

1. Read Colossians 3:1-17. What are some behaviors Paul calls for us to "put to death" once we have been raised with Christ?

_____

_____

2. How does the passage encourage us to live once we are made alive in Christ?

_____

_____

_____

PERSONAL APPLICATION

1. How do you define worship?

_____

_____

2. What are some ways you worship outside of Sunday service? If you don't, why not?

_____

_____

_____

3. List three areas/tasks in your day that in which you can begin to worship.

_____

_____

_____

CLOSING PRAYER

Jesus, you want all of me. And I am all yours. Open my eyes to see that I can worship you in every area in my life. Show me how to glorify you wherever I am and no matter what I'm feeling.

DAY 34

CORPORATE WORSHIP

by Shana Carroll, Director of Worship

SCRIPTURE VERSE

"Come, let us sing for joy to the Lord; let us shout aloud to the Rock of our salvation…Come, let us bow down in worship, let us kneel before the Lord our Maker." Psalm 95:1&6

DEVOTIONAL

Picture this: You walk into church a little late. The music has started. As you look around you see a man with his hands raised. Another kneeling. A woman with her head bowed and hands over her heart. As worship director at CenterPoint, I'm grateful that we have such a wide spectrum of postures during worship and that many in our congregation incorporate their bodies as well as their voices into their praise. When we are passionate about something, many of us respond physically, whether in sports or during worship.

How we express ourselves in Sunday worship is partly a result of our upbringing. Whether you grew up Catholic, Pentecostal, Baptist or unchurched, your worship experience usually dictates your comfort level in your physical response. Our personalities also factor in. Being physically responsive in the midst of others might come easier to an extrovert than to an introvert.

I grew up in a charismatic Lutheran church (I know, what a combo!). I remember wanting to lift my hands in praise to Jesus as I saw so many others doing. But I was terrified. I was worried what my friends would think, worried that it would feel fake. When I finally did, it was such a liberating experience. Raising my hands didn't magically transform me into a better Christian, it just broadened the way I told Jesus I was his, that I was surrendered to him.

These days if I don't have my guitar, I love to assume many different postures during worship depending on the song. *"Waiting here for you, with our hands, lifted high in praise"*—I raise my hands high. *"Create in me a clean heart, O God, and renew a right spirit within me"*—I may assume a more contemplative posture with my head bowed. Dancing can demonstrate joy; a bowed head can show reverence; raised hands can display surrender; and kneeling can represent humility. God created me so I use every part of myself to praise him!

It is easy to dismiss or judge when people assume a worship postures that doesn't suit us. Common judgments include: "That person isn't singing, so they must not be worshipping!" Or, "That person dancing in the front row is such a distraction!" (Confession—I'm usually THAT person in the front row dancing!) And, "People aren't raising their hands, so the worship isn't anointed."

When I start to get judgmental about the people around me in a corporate worship setting, that's usually a sign that my eyes are in the wrong place—anywhere but on Jesus.

Sometimes during worship, you're just not "feeling" it, but you don't want to be inauthentic. I've found that many times in worship we just need to let our body lead and our heart and mind will follow.

BIBLE STUDY

1. What postures of worship do you see in each of the following verses?

• Psalm 47:1

_____

_____

• 2 Samuel 6:14-15

_____

_____

DAY 34

- Matthew 2:11

_____

_____

PERSONAL APPLICATION

1. How do you feel when you see others responding in worship at church?

_____

_____

_____

2. What would you say is your worship posture? Do you feel led to be responsive in a contemplative or expressive way? If so, how?

_____

_____

_____

3. Are you overly conscientious of what others may be thinking when you worship? If so, why?

_____

_____

_____

CLOSING PRAYER

Lord, show me how to respond to you in praise. I admit that I'm sometimes stuck in my own ways. Forgive me for judging my sisters and brothers around me. Help me to not worry about what others are thinking, but to keep my eyes only on you. Amen.

WEEK 6

FOCUS ON DISCIPLINED LIVING

DAY 35

LIVING BY THE SPIRIT

by Steff Eggers, Director of Youth

SCRIPTURE VERSE

"No discipline seems pleasant at the time, but painful. Later on, however, it produces a harvest of righteousness and peace for those who have been trained by it." Hebrews 12:11

DEVOTIONAL

Do you remember when you were young and a parent or teacher asked you to be patient? I do, and it was the *WORST!* Whenever someone used the word "patience" I would cringe. To a kid, patience is a foreign language, *"You mean I have to wait for something that I want right now? Why would I do that?"*

The Bible makes it clear that patience is important. It is one of fruits of the Spirit. Patience, like all of the fruits, is something that comes with discipline.

Let's take a look at Galatians 5:22-23: "But the fruit of the Spirit is love, joy, peace, forbearance *(also referred to as patience)*, kindness, goodness, faithfulness, gentleness and self-control. Against such things there is no law." Do some of these come easier to you than others? Are some more difficult? Have you ever imagined what it would take for you to really pursue each of these fruits? For example, what would it look like if I had more patience with my kids? Or, had more kindness toward strangers?

How can we grow in the fruit of the spirit? First, pray. Ask for God's help, especially with the ones that are tougher for you.

Next, accept the "challenge" of learning these. To truly grasp what kindness is you will need to practice being kind to others. If faithfulness is a struggle, make a plan to be faithful in something whether with your time, your money or another area. If self-control is a challenge, strive to better manage the aspects of your life that are out of your control.

As we put these spiritual disciplines into practice we will see real transformation and growth in ourselves. And others will know we are believers by the fruit of the Spirit in our lives.

Expect it to be a little difficult at first. But just like after a really tough work you see the results, you will see them in your spiritual life as well—and I think you will like what you see!

BIBLE STUDY

1. Read Galatians 5:22-26. Take time to think about the fruit of the Spirit. How can you live by the Spirit and keep in step with the Spirit?

   _____

   _____

   _____

   _____

2. Look again at the list of the fruit of the Spirit. Do you struggle with any of them? Write down the one(s) that you find the most challenging. Take some time to pray and ask God to help you in this area of your life.

   _____

   _____

   _____

   _____

DAY 35

3. Romans 8:5 says, "Those who live according to the flesh have their minds set on what the flesh desires; but those who live in accordance with the Spirit have their minds set on what the Spirit desires." Take a moment to write down some desires you might have. Are they desires from your flesh or from the Spirit?

_____

_____

_____

_____

PERSONAL APPLICATION

Look at what you wrote and take a moment to ask God to help you live more by the Spirit. Ask him to help you keep your eyes on him.

CLOSING PRAYER

God, thank you for your Word, which gives us instructions on how to know you better and follow you more closely. Help me to bear more fruit in my life. Help me especially with the fruit that poses more of a challenge and be close to me in my struggle to attain this fruit. Keep my desires in step with yours. Thank you for what you are doing in my life and what you are yet to do! Amen.

DAY 36

LIVING AS A FAMILY

by Jonelle Wuttke, Director of Children's Ministries

SCRIPTURE VERSE

"Let the little children come to me, and do not hinder them, for the kingdom of heaven belongs to such as these." Matthew 9:14

DEVOTIONAL

God delivered many laws to the people of Israel as recorded in Deuteronomy. CenterPoint's belief that the primary responsibility for children's spiritual wellbeing lies in the home is found in Deuteronomy 6:6-7: "These commandments that I give you today are to be on your hearts. Impress them on your children. Talk about them when you sit at home and when you walk along the road, when you lie down and when you get up." We should use every moment of our day as an opportunity to teach our children about the love of God.

Combining the influence of both family and church in a child's life can have a tremendous impact. At CenterPoint, we refer to this as orange—the love of the family is represented by the color red and the light of the church by yellow, thus combining to create an orange influence. My goal as leader of the children's ministry is to provide parents and caretakers with the resources and tools to practice spiritual disciplines with their children.

Jesus says "Let the little children come to me." Allow these words to sink in. Parents and caretakers are busy people. Children need to be fed, dressed, changed, shuttled, attended to, played with, disciplined and chased after. Practicing spiritual disciplines as a family often falls off the to-do list or feels too overwhelming.

DAY 36

Nevertheless, I encourage you to come before Jesus with your children. Whether you gather together at the table, in the car or by their bedside, pray. Family practice of spiritual disciplines can begin small with prayers of thanks and praise. Integrating conversation with God into your family rhythm will pave the way for worship, scripture and service to become part of your rhythm as well.

Often, society makes the mistake of thinking that children "don't get it" or that faith is too complex and deep for them to grasp. Jesus himself debunks this myth. He knows that a child's heart is the most receptive. When Jesus walked the earth, He welcomed children and blessed them.

Let us follow Jesus' example and, beginning today, pray with and for our children and the children we care for and serve. Begin with prayer. Then God will lead you into other ways to worship and honor him as a family.

BIBLE STUDY

1. Read Deuteronomy 6:1-11. What does the writer say is the most important command that we are to "hold in our heart" and pass down to our children?

_____

_____

_____

_____

2. Read Matthew 22:36-40. Here Jesus states that the most important commandment remains the same. Write it in your own words.

_____

_____

_____

_____

3. What are some ways we can keep this commandment ourselves? How can we teach our children to do the same?

_____

_____

_____

PERSONAL APPLICATION

1. Create a plan for your family that includes:

   - A time for daily prayer
   - A way to study scripture together *(see resources at the end of this book)*
   - Ideas for serving as a family

2. Reflect on your own spirit. Do you believe that you can come to Jesus unhindered because the kingdom of Heaven belongs to you? How can you change your rhythm during these 40 days to accept and pursue this truth?

CLOSING PRAYER

God the Creator, I come before you today and seek love, patience and compassion for the children in my life. I ask that you show me how to love them the way that You do. Lead me as I show them the way to pray. And open my heart to learn from their innocence and unhindered love for You and others. In Jesus' name, Amen.

DAY 37

LIVING SIMPLY

by Brian McMillan, Lead Pastor

SCRIPTURE VERSE

"I know what it is to be in need, and I know what it is to have plenty. I have learned the secret of being content in any and every situation, whether well fed or hungry, whether living in plenty or in want." Philippians 4:12

DEVOTIONAL

I have recently been fascinated by a new trend in housing: micro homes. The average size of these homes is 150 square feet. You read that right. That's the size of some of our closets! And yet people choose to live in these dwellings not necessarily because they cost less but precisely because they are so tiny. These residents have adopted the old adage, less is more. They have chosen fewer possessions and less space to clean so that they can live fuller lives in other areas.

I'm not buying a tiny home anytime soon, but I've been drawn to this phenomenon because it hits on something stirring within me: I believe God has called us to live simpler lives.

Has a generation ever existed that has had access to as much stuff as we do? Our self-indulgent culture is the epitome of consumerism and excess. As a result, our happiness is based on the things we own. We buy the stuff we want, we spend time taking care of it, then we buy things to store our stuff, and on the cycle goes. Our stuff has greatly complicated our lives.

Recently I took inventory of the stockpile of stuff in my own house in order to sell some items on eBay. Seeing it all together was shocking. I spent so much through the years on all my treasured items that I really needed in the moment but used only a few times. And worse, when I tried to sell these precious items, I discovered that they weren't worth anything.

God's conviction started to settle in and I realized: My excessiveness was preventing me from being able to give more and serve more. Instead of saving money or blessing our church or others in need, I'm paying bills. Many of us, instead of spending time with our family or serving God with our time, find ourselves working harder to earn more money to pay for the stuff we have already bought.

We need to start living simpler lives.

Lives that have more freedom.

Lives that find more contentment in Jesus.

I am convinced: A simple life is a contented life. When we choose to live with less, we find freedom. With this freedom, we find our fulfillment and satisfaction in Jesus, in our church community, in the world around us instead of in our stuff.

Friends, truly, less is more.

BIBLE STUDY

1. Read Philippians 4:10-13. When was the last time you were able to be content right where you were?

   _____

   _____

2. How was Paul able to attain this level of contentment?

   _____

   _____

   _____

DAY 37

PERSONAL APPLICATION

Find some items or stuff in your life that you can live without. Give it away or sell it and experience the freedom of living with less.

CLOSING PRAYER

God, please show me if any of my possessions are taking away my freedom. Help me to find greater satisfaction in you, so that whether I am in need or in plenty I can have true contentment. God, help me to live a simpler life. Amen.

DAY 38

LIVING IN GOD'S LOVE

by John Ulin, Pastor of Discipleship and Spiritual Formation

SCRIPTURE VERSE

"My soul thirsts for God, for the living God; When shall I come and appear before God?" Psalm 42:2

DEVOTIONAL

When considering the relationship between our works and God's action, we have to begin with this simple truth: God does not need anything from us. By his very nature God is completely self-sufficient. Paul says this in Acts 17:24-25: "The Lord God, since He is maker of heaven and earth, does not dwell in temples made with hands, nor is he served by human hands as though He needed anything, but He Himself gives life and breath and all things to all people."

What Paul means is that we cannot give God anything that doesn't already belong to him. We offer praise; he gave us our breath with which to praise him. We give a tithe or offering; he gave us the capacity to earn the money (Deuteronomy 8:17-18). It is the same way with every conceivable resource that we have at our disposal (James 1:17). It's all his.

The logical conclusion is that God does not and cannot owe us. We have no leverage to twist his arm or bend his will to our desires. The spiritual disciplines cannot be used to manipulate God. They cannot be used to earn his love or approval, help us make more money, find a spouse or experience healing.

The real goal of the spiritual disciplines must always be to grow closer to

DAY 38

God. Prayer, reading the Bible, worship, simplicity and the other disciplines are intended to be a means of deepening our relationship with God.

In my own life, I have seen that as I strive in these disciplines for the right reasons, God responds. James 4:8 tells us that when we seek after more of God, he draws closer to us. You may not feel it instantly, but it is happening.

Do you see the cycle? As we grow in our love for God, we seek a more significant relationship with him. This desire compels us to pursue him through the disciplines. God responds to our use of the disciplines by strengthening our relationship with him so that we want to pursue him even more. And on and on it goes. Richard Foster put it this way, "If we ever expect to grow [in our relationship with God], we must pay the price of a consciously chosen course of action" (*Celebration of Discipline*, 8).

If we do our part, God is faithful to do his.

BIBLE STUDY

1. Read James 4:8. If God draws near to us when we draw near to him, who limits the intimacy in our relationship? Us or him?

   _____

   _____

   _____

   _____

2. What are some ways in which a more intimate relationship with God would change the way you think, feel and act?

   _____

   _____

   _____

   _____

PERSONAL APPLICATION

1. What are some disciplines you may have under utilized in your spiritual walk? How might these disciplines help you to love God more?

_____

_____

_____

2. Examine your heart: Is your primary motive for praying, reading the Bible and coming to church because you feel guilty if you don't, because you want God's gifts (health, wealth, happiness) or because you want to be closer to him?

_____

_____

_____

3. Have you ever felt let down by God because you didn't receive something you wanted even though you lived "a good Christian life?" What does this say about how you view your relationship with God?

_____

_____

_____

CLOSING PRAYER

God, thank you for the love you've shown me in Christ. I ask that you help me become more grateful for the Gospel and to let that gratitude motivate me to pursue the spiritual disciplines. Lord, help me to always view these disciplines purely as a way to connect with you. I thank you and praise you, in Jesus' name. Amen.

DAY 39

LIVING WITHOUT LEGALISM

by John Ulin, Pastor of Discipleship and Spiritual Formation

SCRIPTURE VERSE

"For I am confident of this very thing, that He who began a good work in you, will perfect it until the day of Christ Jesus." Philippians 1:6

DEVOTIONAL

When I was around 4 years old, my father signed me up for T-ball. T-ball is basically baseball, but you hit the ball off a stand rather than having it pitched. And yet, despite the ball being on a stand, we all still missed it sometimes! Imagine if the coach started yelling at me when I missed the ball or made a mistake on the field. What if he mocked me because I still needed a tee to hit the ball and he didn't? I'd probably feel ashamed, but if my father heard this coach, he would be furious with him, right? Clearly I was just a child and new to the game. If that coach were holding me to an unrealistic standard based on his experience and not mine, it wouldn't be fair.

Thankfully that wasn't my experience with T-ball, but I've seen this mind-set in the church. Whether intentionally or not, many Christians hold new believers and even themselves to an unrealistic standard. As I wrote in one of the other devotionals, we are saved by grace through faith, not because we practice the disciplines, pray or read our Bible regularly. We won't lose our salvation if we miss a devotional day. We should extend grace to ourselves and to others when it comes to our spiritual development.

As veteran Christians, we can mistakenly presume that younger believers must not be trying hard enough because they aren't "more like us" (whatever that means). If only they prayed more, read Scripture, tithed, listened to KLUV, fasted, attended life group and church more often or practiced the other disciplines as consistently as we did, they would be on our level.

Was this Jesus' attitude? Not at all! In Matthew 11:25 Jesus thanks his Father for keeping the secrets of the Kingdom hidden "from the wise and learned and revealing them to the little children." Did you catch that? Jesus called those disciples who had been following him for years "little children." Jesus understood that spiritual growth takes time, even years spent with him. Paul recognized that many of the churches he wrote to were expecting meteoric spiritual growth based on their own effort. He rhetorically asks the Galatians church, "Having been saved by God's Spirit (and not your own works), are you now being perfected by your own works?" (3:3). Paul is essentially saying, "Your didn't get you saved through your own effort, so when did you start thinking it was solely through your own effort that you'd become more like your Savior?" Basically, unrealistic expectations of growth and achievement, like with that T-ball coach, are straight up unbiblical.

Here's what I want you to take away from this: If you're new to the faith or to the disciplines, practice them knowing that your salvation does not depend on them. They are a way for you to connect with the God who has saved you. That's all. Pay attention to how long it takes you to grow so that you will have patience with others when you disciple them. If you've been in the faith for awhile, be a coach that graciously teaches and leads people into a deeper relationship with Christ through the spiritual disciplines.

All those who have put their faith in Christ are on a journey of becoming more like Him. However, it is wrong for us to impose our experiences and our standards on others especially those just starting out. God has a path for all of us to travel. Sometimes we gain ground quickly. Other times the terrain is more difficult and it takes more time. Let us be honest: We didn't start out where we are now. It took time and God's Spirit to get us where we are. And anyway, we are not the standard people should aim for—Jesus is.

May this humbling realization lead us to a deeper gratitude for God's grace that yields in us greater patience for our brothers and sisters in Christ.

DAY 39

BIBLE STUDY

Read Matthew 23:1-6.

1. List the reasons Jesus is upset with the scribes and Pharisees in verse 4.

_____

_____

_____

_____

2. How can Jesus say in verse 3 that the Pharisees know the right things to do, but don't do them? Weren't the Pharisees praying (v. 5) and studying God's Word (v. 6-7)?

_____

_____

_____

PERSONAL APPLICATION

1. Do you know someone who can help you grow in your practice of a discipline? Ask them if they would be willing to check up on you from time to time and help you along the way.

2. Is there a discipline that you feel you would be able to help someone develop? If so, ask that person if they would be interested in your help.

CLOSING PRAYER

Heavenly Father, I thank you for your patience and your grace. I want to be more like your Son and trust that if I pursue you with the disciplines in this book, you will perfect the work you started. As I grow more like Jesus, help me to show others the grace and patience he showed his disciples. For your name and your glory, amen.

DAY 40

A DICIPLINED LIFESTYLE

by Brian McMillan, Lead Pastor

SCRIPTURE VERSE

"Do you not know that in a race all the runners run, but only one gets the prize? Run in such a way as to get the prize." 1 Corinthians 9:24

DEVOTIONAL

I thoroughly enjoy running races. I recently finished the NYC marathon for the second year in a row. My favorite part of a race is the moment I cross the finish line and someone is waiting with a big smile to put a medal around my neck. In that moment I know I did it—I finished something that I set my mind to accomplish. I will spend a few minutes reflecting on the hours of training that got me to this point. And I actually feel a little melancholy because after all the time invested, the moment is now over.

But I don't stay in this place for too long because I know there's more to come. I still have many races ahead of me. More medals to earn. And many more hours of hitting the pavement training.

If I stop running after just one race, I would quickly become lazy. I would gain weight. I would get sluggish. My cholesterol would increase. My energy would decrease. No, I must keep running.

Friends, take a moment to savor what you have done over the last 40 days. Reflect on what you have learned. Be proud of your consistency, even if you took a few days off here and there. But, *don't stop now!* The purpose of these 40 days was to give you the tools to live your faith on your own. To develop healthy patterns and habits. I pray that God has birthed a new expectation

DAY 40

in your hearts and a new idea of what it means to have a relationship with God. And I hope that now you can't imagine life with out it.

On Day 1, I wrote about the need to get a clear view of God's picture for your life. Now that you see him better, now that he is coming into focus, why revert to a spiritual blur? The clearer God becomes in your life, the more your life will make sense. As we bring God into focus, we see everything with a new clarity—our families, our careers, our relationships. As our view of God becomes more focused, so do our lives.

Stay Focused!

BIBLE STUDY

1. Read 1 Corinthians 9:24-27. What does it look like for you to train for this spiritual race?

_____

_____

_____

_____

2. What is the prize that Paul is talking about?

_____

_____

_____

PERSONAL APPLICATION

Plan NOW what you will do tomorrow. You may schedule a media fast or take time to look at the Bible reading plan we have included. But whatever you choose, make sure you do it tomorrow. Carry on the momentum!

CLOSING PRAYER

God, help me to continue pursuing you. Help me to run in such a way as to get the prize. God, I love you. Thank you for all the various avenue I have to get to know you and grow in you. God, I give my life to you. Direct my path. I love you. Amen.

READ THE BIBLE IN 365 DAYS

For additional Bible reading plans, go to www.biblestudytools.com.
You may choose to only read the New Testament Chapters for the first year.

- DAY 1: GEN 1-3; MATT 1
- DAY 2: GEN 4-6; MATT 2
- DAY 3: GEN 7-9; MATT 3
- DAY 4: GEN 10-12; MATT 4
- DAY 5: GEN 13-15; MATT 5:1-26
- DAY 6: GEN 16-17; MATT 5:27-48
- DAY 7: GEN 18-19; MATT 6:1-18
- DAY 8: GEN 20-22; MATT 6:19-34
- DAY 9: GEN 23-24; MATT 7
- DAY 10: GEN 25-26; MATT 8:1-17
- DAY 11: GEN 27-28; MATT 8:18-34
- DAY 12: GEN 29-30; MATT 9:1-17
- DAY 13: GEN 31-32; MATT 9:18-38
- DAY 14: GEN 33-35; MATT 10:1-20
- DAY 15: GEN 36-38; MATT 10:21-42
- DAY 16: GEN 39-40; MATT 11
- DAY 17: GEN 41-42; MATT 12:1-23
- DAY 18: GEN 43-45; MATT 12:24-50
- DAY 19: GEN 46-48; MATT 13:1-30
- DAY 20: GEN 49-50; MATT 13:31-58
- DAY 21: EX 1-3; MATT 14:1-21
- DAY 22: EX 4-6; MATT 14:22-36
- DAY 23: EX 7-8; MATT 15:1-20
- DAY 24: EX 9-11; MATT 15:21-39
- DAY 25: EX 12-13; MATT 16
- DAY 26: EX 14-15; MATT 17
- DAY 27: EX 16-18; MATT 18:1-20
- DAY 28: EX 19-20; MATT 18:21-35
- DAY 29: EX 21-22; MATT 19
- DAY 30: EX 23-24; MATT 20:1-16
- DAY 31: EX 25-26; MATT 20:17-34
- DAY 32: EX 27-28; MATT 21:1-22
- DAY 33: EX 29-30; MATT 21:23-46
- DAY 34: EX 31-33; MATT 22: 1-22
- DAY 35: EX 34-35; MATT 22:23-46
- DAY 36: EX 36-38; MATT 23:1-22
- DAY 37: EX 39-40; MATT 23:23-39
- DAY 38: LEV 1-3; MATT 24:1-28
- DAY 39: LEV 4-5; MATT 24:29-51
- DAY 40: LEV 6-7; MATT 25:1-30
- DAY 41: LEV 8-10; MATT 25:31-46
- DAY 42: LEV 11-12; MATT 26:1-25
- DAY 43: LEV 13; MATT 26:26-50
- DAY 44: LEV 14; MATT 26:51-75
- DAY 45: LEV 15-16; MATT 27:1-26
- DAY 46: LEV 17-18; MATT 27:27-50
- DAY 47: LEV 19-20; MATT 27:51-66
- DAY 48: LEV 21-22; MATT 28
- DAY 49: LEV 23-24; MARK 1:1-22
- DAY 50: LEV 25; MARK 1:23-45
- DAY 51: LEV 26-27; MARK 2
- DAY 52: NUM 1-2; MARK 3:1-19
- DAY 53: NUM 3-4; MARK 3:20-35
- DAY 54: NUM 5-6; MARK 4:1-20
- DAY 55: NUM 7-8; MARK 4:21-41
- DAY 56: NUM 9-11; MARK 5:1-20
- DAY 57: NUM 12-14; MARK 5:21-43
- DAY 58: NUM 15-16; MARK 6:1-29
- DAY 59: NUM 17-19; MARK 6:30-56
- DAY 60: NUM 20-22; MARK 7:1-13
- DAY 61: NUM 23-25; MARK 7:14-37
- DAY 62: NUM 26-28; MARK 8
- DAY 63: NUM 29-31; MARK 9:1-29
- DAY 64: NUM 32-34; MARK 9:30-50
- DAY 65: NUM 35-36; MARK 10:1-31
- DAY 66: DEUT 1-3; MARK 10:32-52
- DAY 67: DEUT 4-6; MARK 11:1-18
- DAY 68: DEUT 7-9; MARK 11:19-33
- DAY 69: DEUT 10-12; MARK 12:1-27
- DAY 70: DEUT 13-15; MARK 12:28-44
- DAY 71: DEUT 16-18; MARK 13:1-20
- DAY 72: DEUT 19-21; MARK 13:21-37
- DAY 73: DEUT 22-24; MARK 14:1-26
- DAY 74: DEUT 25-27; MARK 14:27-53
- DAY 75: DEUT 28-29; MARK 14:54-72
- DAY 76: DEUT 30-31; MARK 15:1-25
- DAY 77: DEUT 32-34; MARK 15:26-47
- DAY 78: JOSH 1-3; MARK 16
- DAY 79: JOSH 4-6; LUKE 1:1-20
- DAY 80: JOSH 7-9; LUKE 1:21-38
- DAY 81: JOSH 10-12; LUKE 1:39-56
- DAY 82: JOSH 13-15; LUKE 1:57-80
- DAY 83: JOSH 16-18; LUKE 2:1-24
- DAY 84: JOSH 19-21; LUKE 2:25-52
- DAY 85: JOSH 22-24; LUKE 3
- DAY 86: JUDG 1-3; LUKE 4:1-30

RESOURCES

Many resources are available at www.amazon.com, and some are for sale at our Family Resource Center located in the lower lobby of CenterPoint.

ONLINE RESOURCES

To learn more about the verses you are reading, use the following websites:

- *Biblehub.com,* for multiple translations, original languages, commentaries, word studies

- *Biblestudytools.com,* for Bible reading plans, videos, devotionals

- *Blueletterbible.org,* for articles, Bible dictionaries, audio and video commentaries

SPIRITUAL FORMATION

- *Contemplative Prayer,* by Thomas Merton

- *The Cloister Walk,* by Kathleen Norris

- *With Open Hands,* by Henri Neuwen

- *Sabbath as Resistance: Saying No to the Culture of Now,* by Walter Bruggemann

DAILY DEVOTIONS

- *Streams in the Desert,* by Lettie Cowman

- *A Year with God: Living Out the Spiritual Disciplines,* by Julia Roller & Richard Foster

- *Prayer with the Psalms,* by Eugene Peterson

PARENTS

- *Parenting Beyond Your Capacity*, by Reggie Joiner and Carey Nieuwhof

- *Playing for Keeps/Losing Your Marbles*, by Reggie Joiner and Kristin Ivy

- *The Space Between*, by Walt Mueller

- *99 Thoughts for Parents of Teenagers: Truth from Parents Who Have Been There*, by Walt Mueller

KIDS

- *The NIrV Adventure Bible*, by Lawrence O. Richards

- *The Jesus Storybook Bible*, by Sally Lloyd-Jones

- *Jesus Calling: 365 Devotions for Kids*, by Sarah Young

- *Know God: A 28 day devotional*, available in lobby

YOUTH

- *99 Thoughts on the Creator*, by Jason Ostrander

- *99 Thoughts on Raising Your Parents*, by Liesl and Max Oestreicher

- *10 Minute Moments*, by Joshua Griffin

NOTES

NOTES

NOTES

NOTES

NOTES

NOTES

CPSIA information can be obtained at www.ICGtesting.com
Printed in the USA
BVOW08s0437180315

392111BV00006B/16/P